DRAWING SCENERY

for Theater, Film and Television

RICH ROSE

BETTERWAY BOOKS

Cincinnati, Ohio

METRIC CONVERSION CHART

To Convert	To	Multiply by
Inches	Centimeters	2.54
Centimeters	Inches	0.4
Feet	Centimeters	30.5
Centimeters	Feet	0.03

98   97   96   95   94   5   4   3   2   1

Library of Congress Cataloging in Publication Data
Rose, Rich.
     Drawing scenery for theater, film and television / by Rich Rose. — 1st ed.
          p.   cm.
     Includes index.
     ISBN 1-55870-348-9
     1. Theaters — Stage-setting and scenery. 2. Motion pictures — Setting and scenery. 3. Television — Stage-setting and scenery. 4. Drawing — Technique. I. Title.
PN2091.S8R586   1994
792'.025 — dc20   94-7095
                                                                                            CIP

Edited by Hilary Swinson
Interior and cover design by Paul Neff

TO CAMERON

ACKNOWLEDGMENTS

I would like to thank George Jenkins, Matt Flynn and Jonathan Bourne. Without their help much of this book would not have been possible.

Contents

1

The Sketch

THE DESIGN PROCESS

Unlike the lighting designer who must talk his or her way through design ideas with the director and other designers, the scenic designer can present more concrete evidence of what shape the set might eventually take. This evidence can take the form of a model, rendering or sketch, depending on the stage of the discussions, the complexity of the design or the preference of the designer. There is certainly nothing like a three-dimensional model for communicating the true volume and relationships of elements in the performance space. Spatial correlations can be confusing or difficult to explain in the two-dimensional world of the rendering. But there is nothing like a well-rendered sketch, with its ability to show atmosphere and light, for conveying the mood and textures of a scene.

The sketch is used in the earliest stages of a collaborative design process to illustrate preliminary thoughts about the design for the director or other designers. Because no time-consuming painting or model building is involved, sketching the design can be quite quick. This puts the emphasis on the design rather than the technique. In the early drafts, the black-and-white sketch can be relatively small, making it perfect for quick modifications and even faxing to the director or other designers across town or across the country. Since the sketch is modest in size, it is fairly easy to modify or redesign and quickly prepare a new sketch for the next meeting. As the design evolves so will the sketch — in detail, size and complexity. Eventually you will need to convert the sketch into a rendering or model.

In my own work I sometimes use computers to help illustrate true three-dimensional wireframe perspective "models" of the design. I can show the design from different angles to help illustrate what the production will look like from various seats in the audience. New PC-based rendering programs, such as Autodesk's *3D Studio*, can yield photorealistic renderings from these wire-frame "models." The cost of such systems is beginning to be within reach of many designers. No matter how much I use computers during the design process, however, I begin all my designs with a sketch.

The sketch is the first tool that most designers use in the mechanics of the design process. Designers with computer systems and even avid model builders oftentimes start with a thumbnail sketch before picking up foam core board and balsa wood. Experienced designers who are intuitive drawers can achieve a final sketch in one session (or over a period of two or three sessions) without the need for a sketch development technique. For the designer who is not yet at that level of experience, this book shows systems for developing a sketch.

SKETCH DEVELOPMENT TECHNIQUES

The methods and techniques in this book are simplified variations of classic perspective — which this book will not even begin to encompass. During the years I have taught, I have discovered that classic perspective, while the only true technique for achieving an accurate sketch, is often lost on students and novice designers who don't have the patience for its laundry list of rules to remember and follow. Instead, this book presents the procedures that my students and I have been using for a number of years. Not all of them "click" with all people, but it is rare that at least one technique doesn't do the trick.

Before exploring these methods, the book will take you through a perspective primer. Here the basic principles of perspective will be explained without delving into classic perspective. The success of the remainder of the book rests on your understanding this chapter's basic ideas about perceiving the three-dimensional world. After exploring the fundamentals you will investigate several modified-perspective techniques. Two involve transforming orthographic floor plans into perspective floor plans. One uses a connect-the-dots approach to develop a sketch, and the other uses a perspective grid mode.

The next technique involves building an approximation of your set in model form. This won't be the conventional model since you will build it out of found objects. The assemblage is "built" in only a few minutes and then the sketching begins.

If you are good at thumbnail sketches and break out in a rash at the thought of perspective technique — any perspective technique — then chapter seven is for you. This chapter looks at developing the design through a thumbnail sketch and then presents a technique for enlarging and refining your drawing. I have found this technique quite successful for those who have trouble visualizing in three dimensions or for those who simply can't grasp the logic of perspective.

Sketching for the camera lens view has a unique set of issues. Chapter eight guides you through a remarkable technique that accurately shows what the camera will see from any position. The outcome of the sketch varies depending on the type of lens you use. The method also considers the curvature of the lens as it tends to distort the image. This technique was handed down to me by Academy-Award-winning production designer George Jenkins (*All the President's Men*, *The China Syndrome*, *The Best Years of Our Lives*) with the help of UCLA graduate student Matt Flynn.

The examples and explanations in the book are geared toward sets with walls. For sets that have few or no walls, or set pieces that aren't planar, we will look at ways of modifying the techniques presented in the earlier chapters. You will also glean some hints for sketching foliage, figures (for purposes of referencing scale) and materials. You'll learn to draw brick, block, marble, wood, glass, and other surface textures. These realistically rendered surfaces and plants will help your sketch to convey your design proposal to others as well as help you fully fathom the implications of your design choices.

In successive pages you will also learn to shade your set. Shading contributes atmosphere to your design, and with it you control the spirit of the scene that you are sketching. Gradations of light and shadow improve the physical sense of the sketch and the viewer's three-dimensional perception. All of this creates a presentation that allows the director and other designers to key off of the tonality that you have set up and use it as inspiration for their own directoral or design departures.

Later chapters will survey the preparatory stages leading to an eventual rendering that you might undertake. You will see how to preserve your sketch, transfer it to watercolor paper, or even transfer it to felt-marker paper to create a black-and-white marker sketch or a full-color marker rendering. Chapter fourteen presents an easy method of figuring out the best matt framing aspect ratio and tips for cutting the matt.

The book concludes with examples of sketches (or "sketchy" renderings) that exhibit a range of style and technique. Use these illustrations as another source of ideas and techniques or simply as inspiring points of departure for your next sketch.

SKETCH DIARY

If drawing scenery intimidates you at all, remember that no one started out drawing beautiful sketches on the very first try. Like the body builder who achieves a winning physique after years of weight lifting — one more pound and one more day at a time — you can become proficient at sketching with lots of practice. The body builder spends a little time each day going through a weight-lifting routine. You can build your drawing "muscles" if you will spend just a little time each day drawing in a sketchbook.

A sketch diary is nothing more than the equivalent of weight training. You aren't trying to crank out a rendering or meet a deadline. You are sketching to train your drawing muscles and "work out" issues involved with drawing different types of objects. You can draw whatever you like in your diary as long as you draw something every day. You should start each session by drawing objects that are easy for you and don't require much motivation. I usually suggest that my students draw their television — while they are watching it — as a first project. The next day you might spread out to things near the television, such as a bookcase, aquarium or desk. Become a little more adventurous each day and begin to draw things that challenge you. These will ultimately be the objects that you are most interested in drawing because of their complexity. You will eventually find them to be some of your best drawings as well. Don't worry what anything looks like, and don't show your diary to anyone. Remember no one looks like Arnold Schwarzenegger after one week, and your drawings won't look like Norman Rockwell's in that time period either. It doesn't matter what your sketches look like. No one will see them so don't bother criticizng them. Just find the satisfaction in slowly becoming a better drawer. With continuous practice your sketches will be as good as anyone's.

Although it doesn't matter what you draw, what follows is a list and some examples of sketch diary subjects in a suggested order. Begin each session with warm-up exercises to get your hand moving over the entire paper. Some suggestions:

- Geometric objects (a star in a circle in a square, etc.)
- Boxes over grid lines

Sketch diary assignment suggestions:

- Boxes (tissue, cereal, cartons, etc.)
- Television
- Items near the television (aquarium, bookcase, desk, etc.)
- Radio

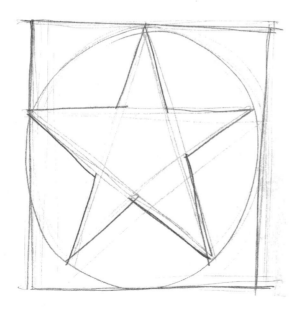

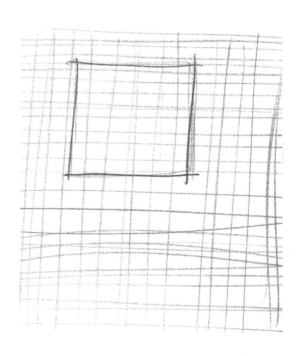

- Chair
- Rectangular exterior architecture
- Cylindrical object (wastebasket, pipe, bucket, etc.)
- Still life of cylindrical objects
- Cloth over cylindrical object
- Cloth over objects
- Draped fabric or clothing
- Your hand
- Shoe
- Lamp
- Bicycle
- Iron on ironing board
- Complex exterior architecture
- Tree
- Living room
- A flower
- Floral still life
- Garage tools still life
- Kitchen utensils still life
- Close-up corner of a car detail
- Landscape setting (in a park, a tree-lined street, etc.)
- Bare foot
- Telephone
- A friend
- Rocks (still life or natural setting)
- Drapery

This list should get you started. It contains a month's supply of ideas. For the next month you may want to repeat this list and then compare the drawings. The improvement will amaze you and inspire you to keep pushing ahead. Be creative and develop your own list for future months. The chapters ahead will get you pointed in the right direction toward determining a simplified *perspective* technique that works for you. The technical skill involved in the *drawing* technique is completely up to you. Keep your sketch diary active and I guarantee that you will master the keys to a successful sketch.

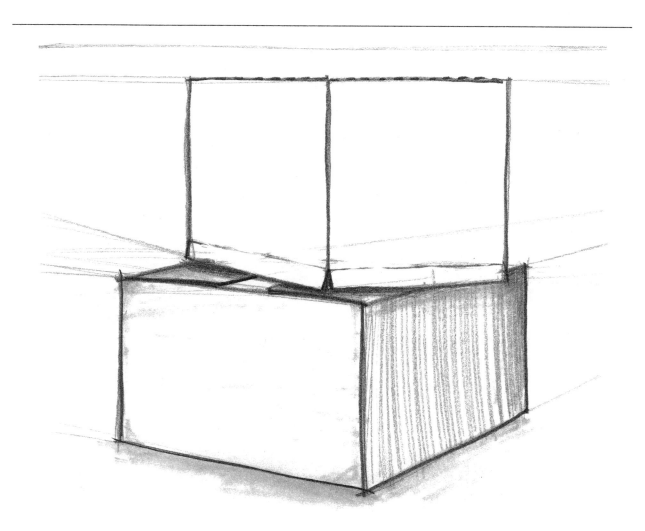

The Sketch

Drawing Scenery for Theater, Film and Television

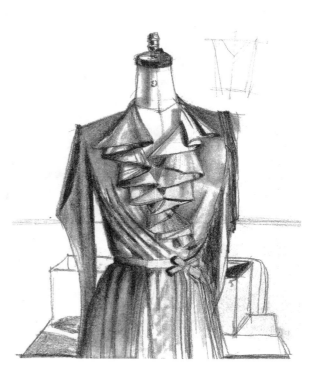

2

Materials and Tools

EMPHASIZE QUALITY

When you think of sketching, you probably think of a pencil, some paper and perhaps an eraser. When it comes to sketching a set design, however, you may want to communicate a fairly accurate description of the stage space. Accuracy requires precision. To be precise you will need to use some tools. You don't need to spend a fortune. Prices can vary, so shop around. Don't buy a tool simply because it is the cheapest either. A tool might look as good as its more expensive shelf mate, but it may not last through the project. If in doubt, ask the sales help in the art supply store for advice on quality tools and materials. You will never go wrong by purchasing the highest quality tools and materials you can afford.

THE BASIC SETUP

You will need a drawing table, a place to sit and something in which to store your equipment and materials. Recommendations: Stay away from tables that shake a lot. When shopping around test each table for sturdiness and stability. Buy a soft plastic drawing surface to cover your tabletop, such as a Borco brand drawing surface. If you have the money, get a padded swivel stool with an adjustable seat and back. Get two swing-arm lamps that use incandescent bulbs. Stay away from fluorescent lights—they don't show color accurately. A tabouret such as that shown in the sketch below will hold most of your materials easily.

DRAWING AND ERASING

Here is a list of the basic tools you might need for
sketching your designs. Recommendations: Unless
you want to completely stay away from ink, get everything on this page: #2 pencil, very soft drawing pencil, finepoint pen, "Sharpie" pen, stomp and plastic
eraser. Make sure your stomp is not the hollow type;
it should be solid all the way through.

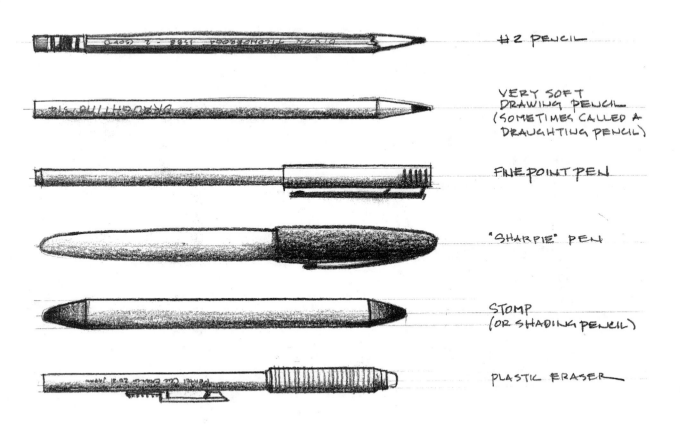

#2 PENCIL

VERY SOFT
DRAWING PENCIL
(SOMETIMES CALLED A
DRAUGHTING PENCIL)

FINEPOINT PEN

"SHARPIE" PEN

STOMP
(OR SHADING PENCIL)

PLASTIC ERASER

MEASURING, CUTTING AND STRAIGHT LINES

Some of the methods in this book require working in scale. For that you will need a scale ruler. Recommendations: Make sure the ruler has ¼″ and ½″ scales on it. Get a metal edged ruler for cutting with a matt knife. For parallel lines you will need a T-square. If you can afford to substitute the T-square with a parallel rule, do so. They sell for about one dollar per inch (36″ = about $36) and are easier to use than a T-square.

SCALE RULE

MATT KNIFE

METAL EDGED RULER (18")

falcon

T-SQUARE

TRIANGLE, TAPE AND SHARPENER

There is no substitute for a triangle when it comes to drawing nonparallel straight lines. Shown here is a 30-60-90° triangle. Recommendations: Get drafting "dots" rather than tape. They don't curl up under the T-square as easily as tape does. An electric sharpener will speed up your drawing sessions. You'll be surprised to find how cheap a battery-operated model is.

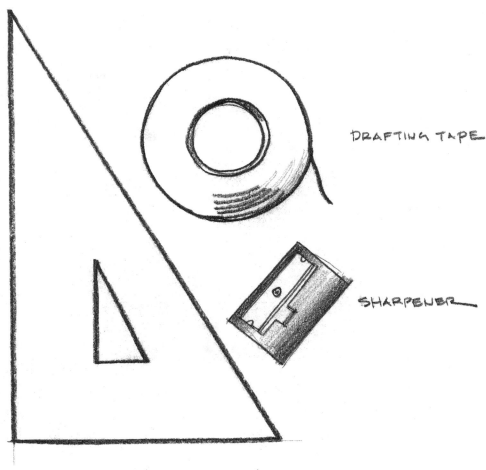

DRAFTING TAPE

SHARPENER

TRIANGLE (TALL & SKINNY)

PAPER

Shown here are three kinds of paper for sketching:
sketch, newsprint and tracing. Which to use? Try all
three if you can, and see which feels best to you.
Recommendations: I prefer newsprint (or bond) for
two reasons: (1) the tooth — newsprint is rough,
therefore it "grabs" the graphite so the lines flow
easily; (2) the price — it's quite cheap. Tracing paper
is good for evolving a design. If you aren't completely
happy with the first sketch, place a sheet of tracing
paper over it. Copy what you like and change what
you don't like.

FIXATIVE AND CLEANER

Spraying a little fixative on your drawing will keep the graphite from smearing. A household spray cleaner, such as 409 or Fantastik, will clean your table and your tools with ease. Recommendations: Don't use soap and water to clean your drawing table surface. Drafting tape and dots don't stick well to tables cleaned with soap and water.

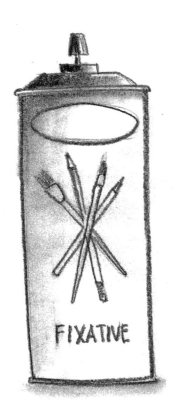

MATT BOARD

You will need matt board to put a border around your designs for more formal presentations. Recommendations: Buy black board. It is neutral and therefore will not compete with the design. If you have any left over it can be used for future presentations.

BLACK OR GREY
MATT BOARD

MARKERS

Markers are optional but they can be an effective way of depicting subtle tone variation and shadow. Using grey markers is explored in a later chapter.

PORTFOLIO

Get a portfolio for storing your drawings. Portfolios will range in price and quality—from cheap cardboard to elaborate and expensive leather.

GREY FELT MARKERS

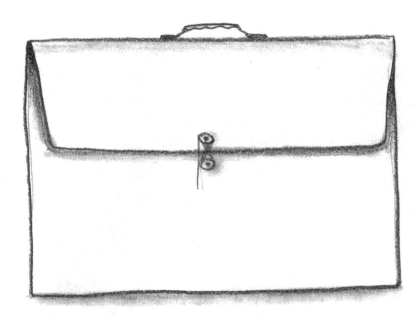

SKETCH PORTFOLIO
FOR STORAGE

DRAFTING BRUSH AND
TRANSFER PAPER

A drafting brush will wipe erasures away from your
drawing without smearing the sketch. Transfer paper
is a must when it comes to transferring the sketch to
another surface for rendering in color.

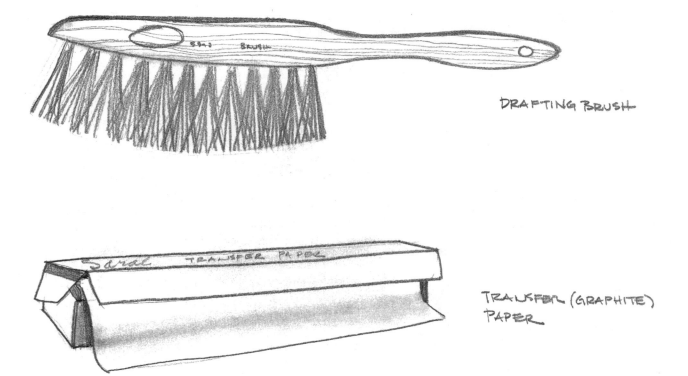

DRAFTING BRUSH

TRANSFER (GRAPHITE)
PAPER

3

Principles of Perspective

PLAYING WITH PERSPECTIVE

You have probably played around with perspective in the past. You might have attempted a drawing like the one on the following page when you began to try perspective drawing as a child. It was a challenge to try to get the drawing to look as three-dimensional as possible. These 3-D-like drawings are called *perspective* drawings. You may very well have been frustrated by trying to make your drawing look natural and realistic. Now that you have assembled the drawing tools and materials you need, and you've done some sketching to warm up, let's take a closer look at just what it was you were trying to accomplish.

A PERSPECTIVE EXAMPLE

All of the elements in this sample fall into two categories: objects with lines that appear to converge at the center of the drawing (and seem to get smaller) and objects with lines that don't converge (yet seem to get smaller). The first category includes the telephone poles, railroad track, and highway and lane stripes. The second category includes the telephone pole, footholds and railroad ties. Even though the ties themselves don't appear to converge, the edges of the ties and an imaginary line that would connect the edges do converge in the center.

That first category includes lines that (if we were to look down on this scene from above) are all parallel and go toward or away from us. These lines are perpendicular to the picture plane. The other lines in this drawing are parallel to the picture plane. They don't go either toward us or away from us.

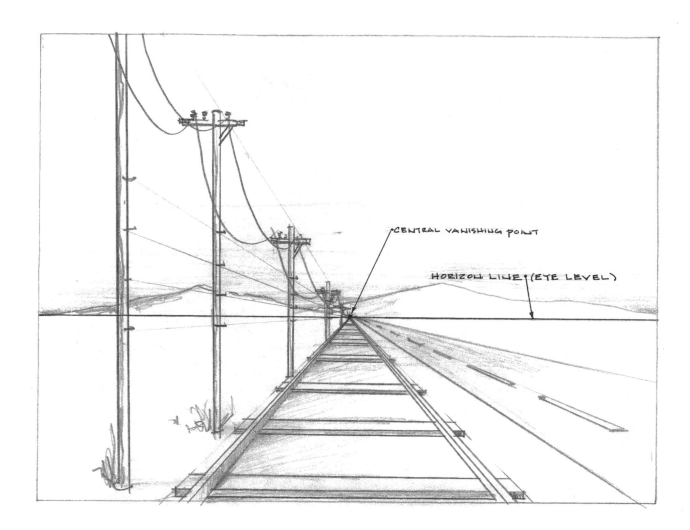

SCHEMATIC

Here is a schematic of the railroad scene. You can
see that the position and size of all of the elements
in the drawing are strongly controlled by a *vanishing
point*. The vanishing point is the point where the
lines converge. (This drawing has one central vanishing point.) The vanishing point lies on the *horizon
line*. The horizon line represents the eye level of the
viewer or creator of the drawing. A drawing can be
sketched at any height by raising or lowering the
horizon line. Drawings with low horizon lines look
up at the set and are quite dramatic. Drawings with
high horizon lines look down and appear to be drawn
from the balcony or control booth. Most scenic
sketches are drawn as if viewed from the eye level
of someone sitting in the middle of the audience.

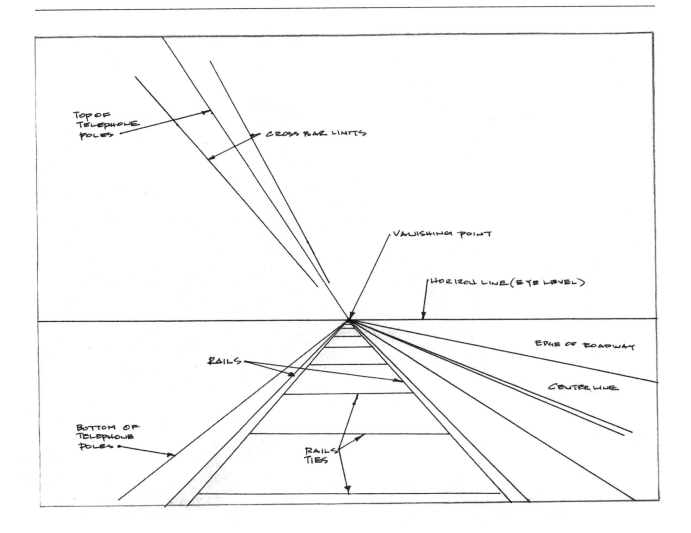

Drawing Scenery for Theater, Film and Television

ONE-POINT PERSPECTIVE

Like the railroad scene before it, this cube illustrates
the basic principles of one-point perspective. The
top of the cube has two edges that are perpendicular
to the picture plane and therefore converge at the
vanishing point. On the other hand, all the lines that
make up the face of the cube are parallel to the picture plane. They are therefore unaffected by the vanishing point. Notice that the cube line is roughly
centered below the vanishing point.

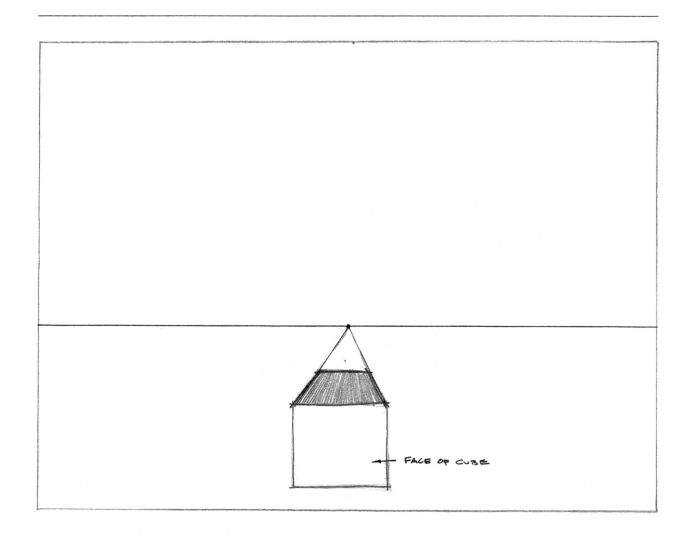

FACE OF CUBE

MOVING THE CUBE

This drawing illustrates what happens when the cube
goes higher or lower than the horizon line (but re-
mains roughly centered on the vanishing point).
Since the horizon line represents eye level, cube *A*
is below the observer. You are looking down on the
top surface of the cube. Cube *C* is higher than the
horizon line. It is above you so you look up to see
the bottom surface. Cube *B* is placed so its middle
straddles the horizon line. Since it is neither above
nor below you, you see neither the top nor the bottom.

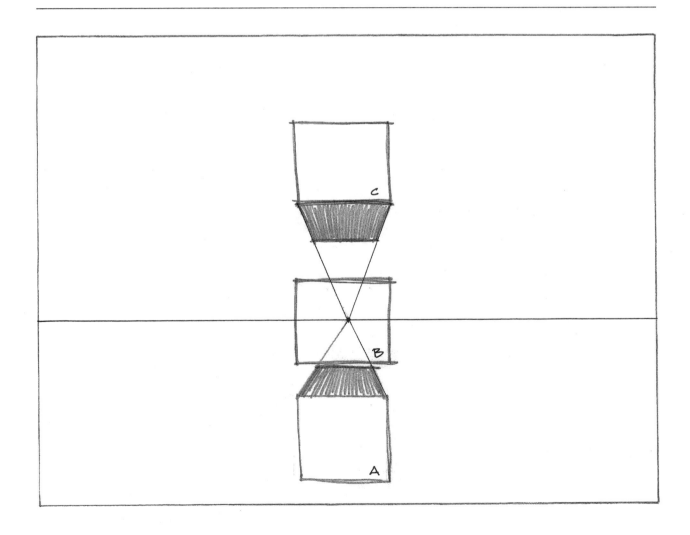

REVEALING SIDES

To the right and left of the original cube tower (tower *B*) are two additional towers (*A* and *C*). The faces of all the cubes are still parallel to the picture plane. Because towers *A* and *C* are to the left and right of the center vanishing point (to the left and right of you) the perspective view reveals an additional side of each cube.

To better understand this, close one eye and hold a cube-like object first in front of you, then above and below you. Move the cube to the left and right, keeping the face of the cube parallel to your face.

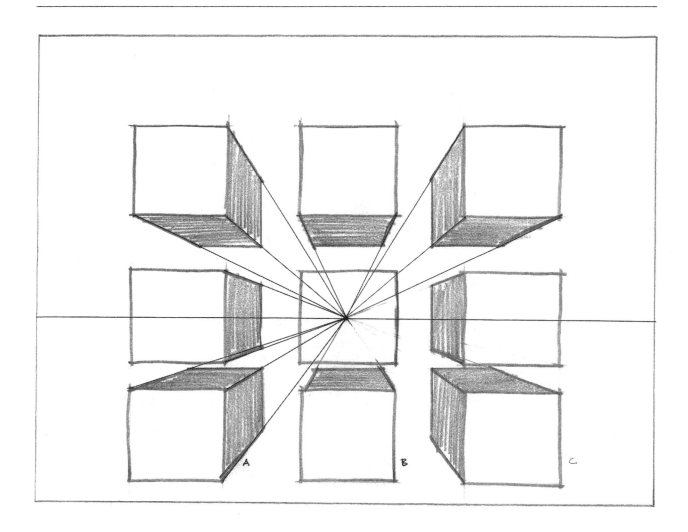

TWO-POINT PERSPECTIVE

Now we change the situation a bit. Our single cube is back, but this time its *edge*—not its face—is on the picture plane. Since only the vertical sides of the cube faces are parallel to the picture plane, the non-parallel sides must converge on the horizon line. But this time there are two vanishing points. This is called *two-point perspective*. Every face that is not parallel to the picture plane has its own vanishing point. Faces that are in planes parallel to each other or are in the same plane share the same vanishing point (see the next example). Since there are two faces in this drawing, you need two vanishing points. Just as in the previous drawings, the top and bottom of this cube are not revealed because the cube straddles the horizon line.

As you may have guessed, there are some rules for establishing these two vanishing points. However, to keep things simple, they have been placed near the edge of the drawing for now.

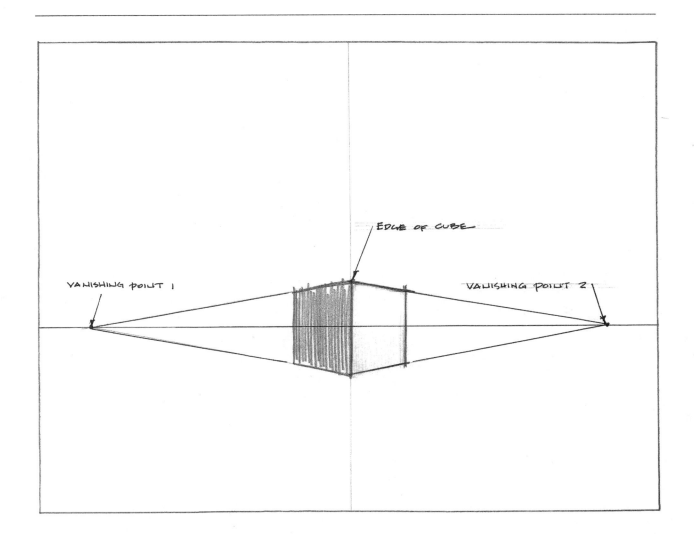

COMMON VANISHING POINTS

This tower of cubes illustrates some more principles of two-point perspective that come into play as the cube is positioned above and below the horizon line. The most basic principle is that the top and bottom of the cube are revealed. More important, you can see how lines that are parallel to each other share a common vanishing point. This is the guiding principle when drawing the back edges of the top and bottom of the cube.

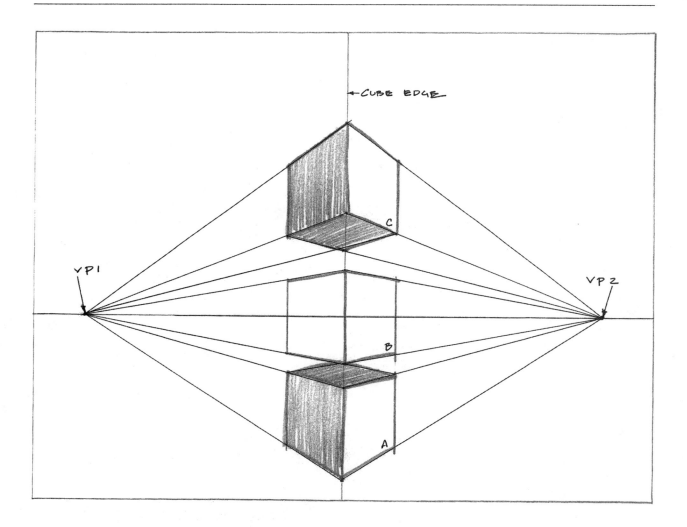

DOMINANT VIEWS

By adding towers *A* and *C*, you can see that the further to the right or left the tower moves, the more that side dominates the view of the cube. This drawing seems to defy the rule that each face not parallel to the picture plane must have its own vanishing point. But if you carefully examine this example and the next one, you will see that since the sides are all parallel, there can be only two vanishing points.

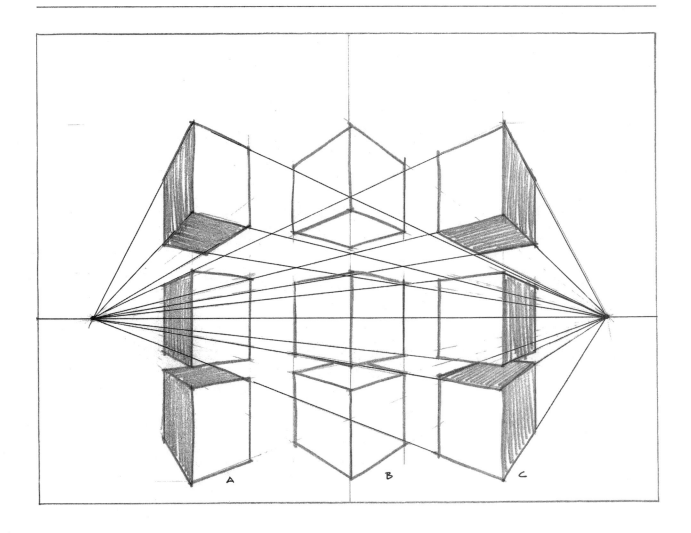

FLOOR PLAN VIEWS

This drawing shows the floor plan setups of each example in this chapter. The fifth plan represents the setup in the next example. Notice that unlike the other setups, the cubes are not perfectly aligned with parallel sides.

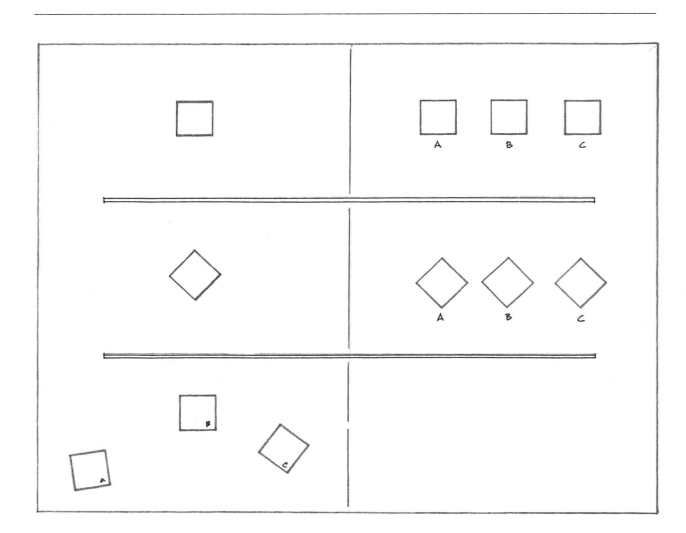

MULTI-POINT PERSPECTIVE

Again, *every face that is not parallel to the picture plane has its own vanishing point*. Cube *B* has been placed so its face is parallel to the picture plane. Whenever this special case occurs in a drawing, a center (center of the entire drawing and on the horizon line) vanishing point is established for *all* such objects. Consequently, there are rules that must be observed when establishing all the other vanishing points. More about that later.

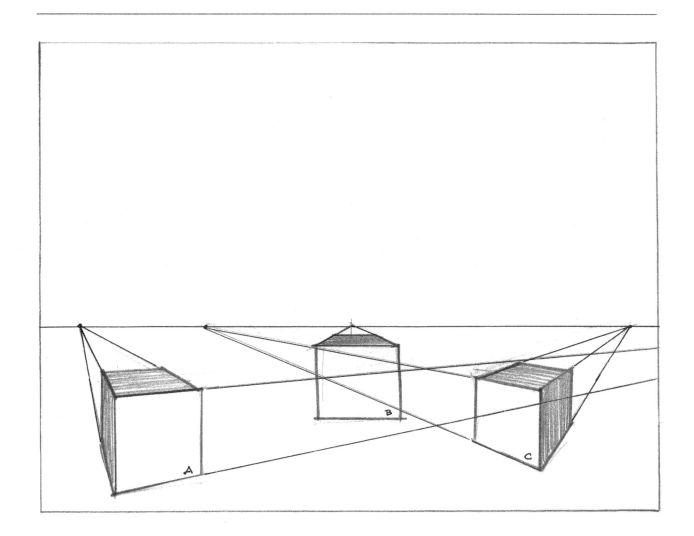

4

Connect-the-Dots Method

EASY TECHNIQUE, GREAT RESULTS

I call this first modified-perspective method the "connect-the-dots" method. (The reason for this name will soon become apparent.) I have had much success in my classes getting students to use this method. You will need a piece of paper as long as the height of your drawing table. Turn it so the longer side is vertical. On the top half of the sheet you will draw the floor plan of your design. The bottom half of the sheet is where you will draw the perspective sketch of your set design. In no time at all, your design will take shape without the words *mechanical perspective* ever being mentioned.

BOX SET

This is an example of a walled "box" set on a 40′ proscenium stage. However, the technique will also work if there are no walls and no proscenium. In that case, you should draw imaginary walls and an imaginary proscenium where real ones might be. This part of the drawing is erased (or not transferred) after the drawing is "built."

STEP 1

A   Draw a line down the length of the center of your paper.

B   Draw the proscenium opening. To do this you will need a scale ruler to measure the opening, or you can simply draw people lying head to toe across the proscenium. This latter method allows you to pro-

ceed without bothering with scale and scale rulers. If you already have a scale floor plan, then using a scale rule is your best option. If you don't have such a plan yet, draw as many same-sized people as you need to determine the opening. In this case we are drawing a 40′ opening, so it requires roughly 6½ people who are all 6′ tall. Both methods yield the same results. You really don't need a scale to do this. Just make sure your people aren't too big to fit on the page.

C   Indicate the edge of the stage. In this example, it is 6′ from the proscenium—or the height of one person.

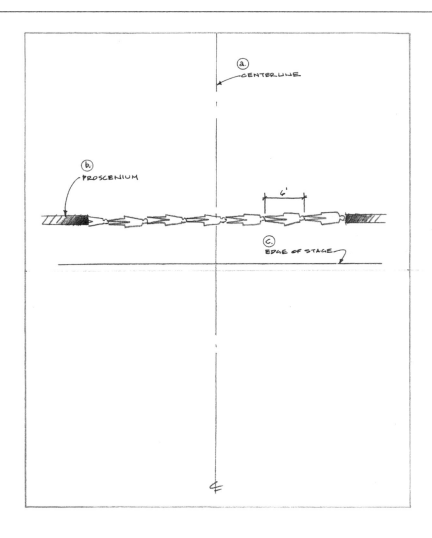

Drawing Scenery for Theater, Film and Television

STEP 2

This next step establishes the position for the set on the stage.

A Draw a line that is roughly 20′ from the edge of the stage and parallel to it. This is an upstage set position guide line. Twenty feet from the edge of the stage is about the limit of the usable acting area. The area upstage of this is too far from the audience for important staging.

B Draw in the extreme audience sight-line seats. If you are not working with a scale floor plan, this can be approximated without too much problem.

C Next, draw the two extreme sight lines from each seat. One line should just touch the stage right pro-

scenium and the other should just touch the stage left proscenium.

The pentagon-shaped area, which was created by the borders of the sight lines and the upstage set position guide line, is usually the best acting area and therefore the place to position the set.

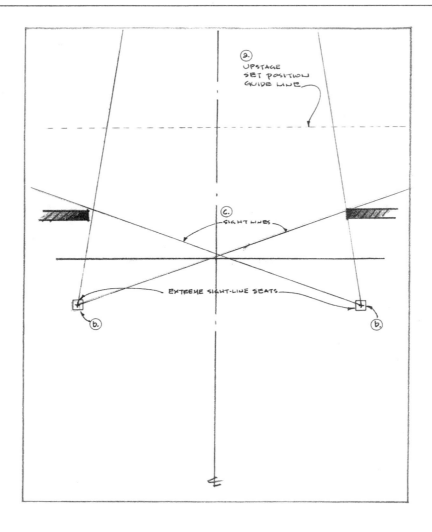

STEP 3

Draw in the floor plan. Now you will begin to develop the sketch itself. This step establishes the proscenium opening from the audience's perspective.

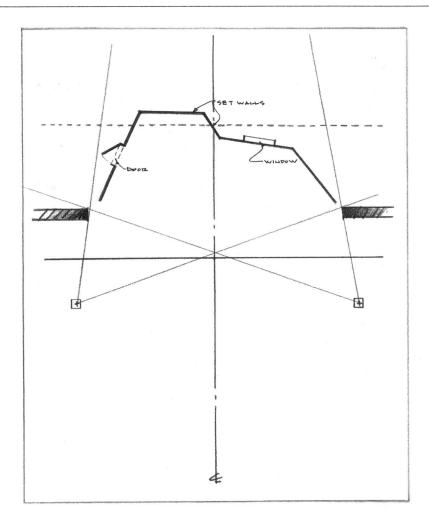

STEP 4

A   Draw a horizontal line near the bottom of the page. This will be the edge of the stage.

B   Draw two vertical lines from the onstage edges of the opening to the bottom of the paper. These will become the right and left sides of the opening.

C   Draw the two bottoms of the proscenium opening. Start them at the vertical line you just drew and then trail off. To place them vertically, draw them above the edge of the stage offset at half the distance of their relationship in the plan above.

D   Draw the top of the proscenium opening. The proscenium opening in this example is 18′ from the stage floor. If you are not using a scale rule, draw

the number of people you need to determine the height — three in this case. Make sure your people are the same size as the ones you created for the plan.

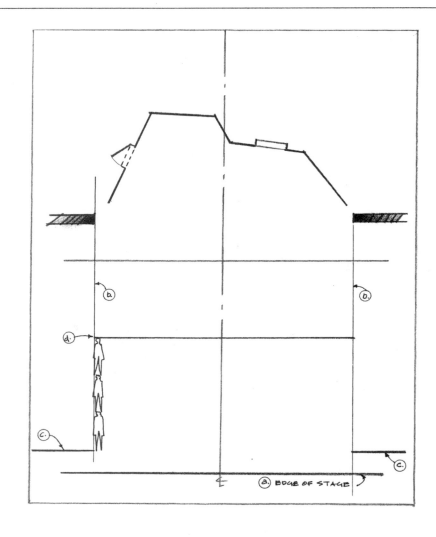

STEP 5

A Draw the horizon line. Place it at half the proscenium height. This is not a hard-and-fast rule, however. The horizon line can be placed virtually anywhere. As I said earlier, placing it higher results in a balcony view; placing it lower heightens the dramatic quality.

B Halfway between the horizon line and the bottom of the proscenium, draw another line that does not go outside the proscenium opening lines. This represents the back of the stage and helps you visualize the placement of set elements in 3-D.

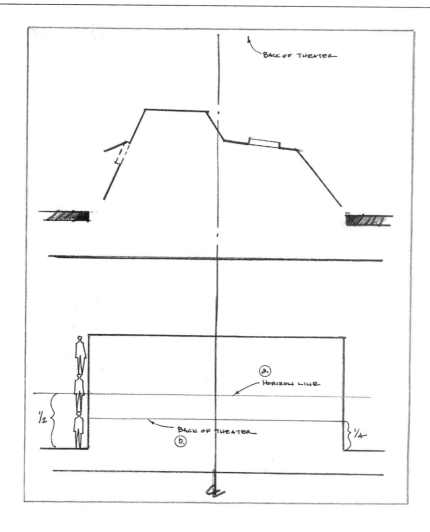

STEP 6

Now you will begin to transfer the set elements from the plan to the sketch. Identify key set elements in the plan above and draw their equivalent positions in the sketch. In this case, draw the walls. Dots numbered 1 to 6 in the plan are at the ends of each wall and highlight this part of the explanation.

A Draw vertical lines from each of the key dots in the plan down to the sketch.

B Estimate the upstage/downstage position for each of these dots in the *sketch*. This distance will be less than it is in the plan because sketches foreshorten. To gauge the dots' positions, determine the plan position *in relation to* the distance of the dots from the back wall or proscenium. (The edge of the page represents the back wall.) For example, dot #3 in the plan is about halfway between the back wall and the proscenium. On the sketch place the dots in the same relation.

C The left/right positions of the dots in the plan appear misaligned. However, they are in the correct position for this connect-the-dots method. In general, the dots #1, 4 and 6 should line up with the vertical guidelines that you drew in step A. Dots #2, 3 and 5 are *onstage* of where you think they should be. For this method to work, the further upstage the dots are, the more you need to cheat them onstage. How much onstage? More if they are way upstage, and less if they aren't as far; more if they are offstage, and less if they are near center.

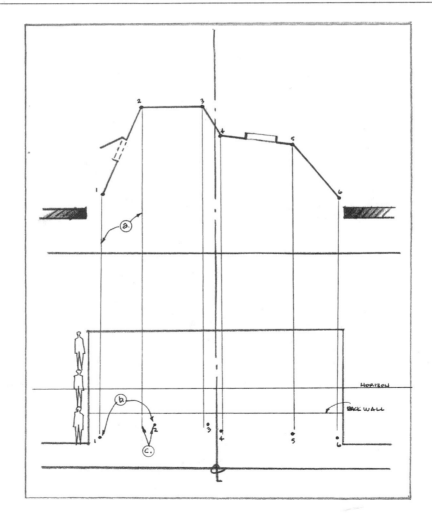

STEP 7

Draw vertical lines up from the dots in the plan.
These represent the edges of the walls.

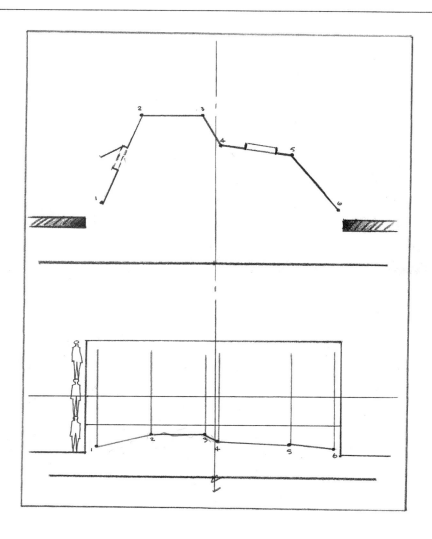

STEP 8

With this step you begin drawing the tops of the walls. Remember that each plane must have its own vanishing point and that elements in parallel planes, or elements in the same plane, share a vanishing point. Both rules will now come into play. Start by establishing the vanishing point for the *A* wall and then work your way around the set.

A Draw a line that *continues the angle* of the *A* wall base until it intersects with the horizon line. This intersection is the vanishing point for the *A* wall and for everything on the wall that is parallel to the bottom of the wall.

B Establish the height of the set. In this case it is 15′ high. If you are using the "people meter," mark the stage right side of the *A* wall at the appropriate person. In this case, it's 2½ people high.

C Draw a line from the height of the set to the *A* vanishing point. You should now have the *A* wall drawn at the correct height and angles.

D The *B* wall is parallel to the picture plane. Remember from the one-point perspective discussion that it has no vanishing point. In cases such as this, draw a horizontal line between the two sides of the wall that connects with the top of the previous wall.

E Repeat step 8A for each of the remaining walls. You can see the completed *C* wall and its vanishing point in this example.

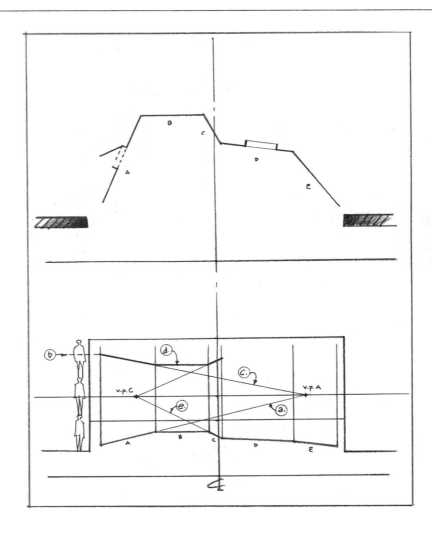

STEP 9

This step completes the process you began in the
previous step. Notice that vanishing points can be
far away from the sketch. It's a good idea to tape
extra pieces of paper to the sketch to accommodate
vanishing points such as these.

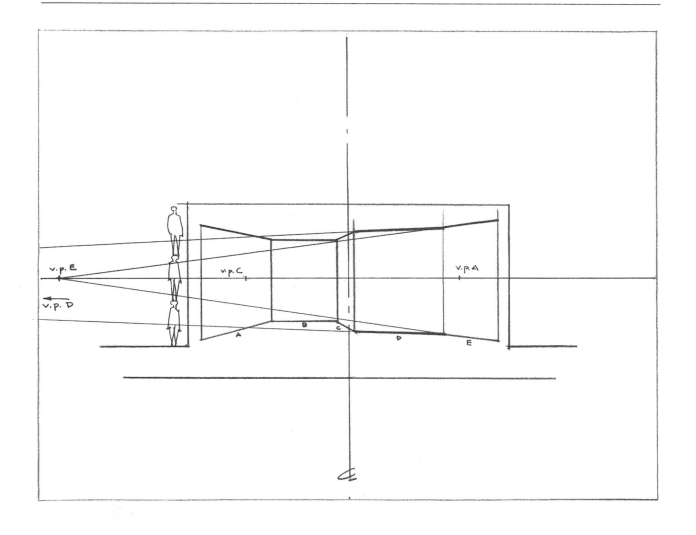

STEP 10

Now that the wall outlines are established, you can draw in the detail using the vanishing points. As long as your vanishing points are clearly labeled as to which wall they belong to, you should have no problem completing the sketch. The door position was drawn by dropping in vertical lines from the plan. The door height was "measured" by determining where 7′ was on the people meter and then drawing a line from the proscenium edge to that wall's vanishing point. An important note: You can only "measure" at the proscenium edge, regardless of whether you have used a scale rule up to this point. Take that measurement around the set (along the vanishing point paths) to where you need it.

Notice that all the elements parallel to the bottom of the flat use the same vanishing point.

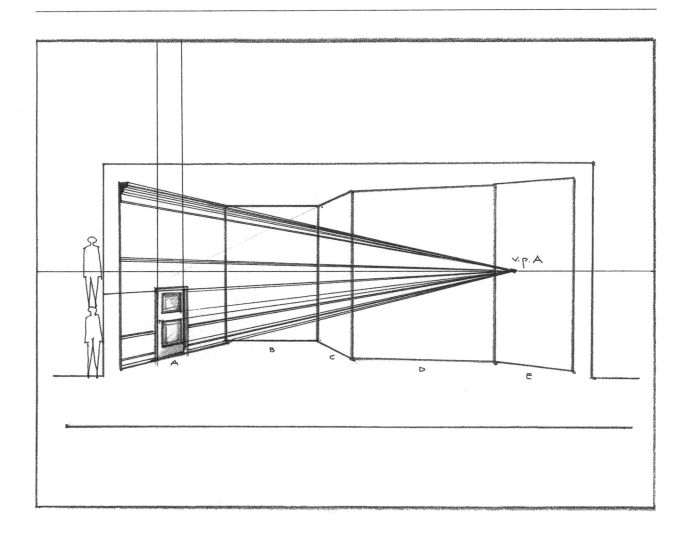

THE FINAL SKETCH

Other elements have been added to complete the sketch. The floorboards are converging on a center vanishing point much like the railroad tracks do. An edge of the apron adds a finishing touch to the bottom of the composition. The black shading around the set represents masking and places the sketch in a theatrical setting.

5

Grid Method

BUILDING A SKETCH

While this modified-perspective method is similar
to the connect-the-dots method, it uses a grid to
transfer the floor plan. This eliminates much of
the guessing involved in positioning set walls in
the plan. As in the previous method, you will need
a piece of paper as long as your drawing table
height. On the top half of the sheet you will draw
a floor plan of your design. This example is of a
walled "box" set on a 27' proscenium stage. The
bottom half of the sheet is where you will build
the sketch.

STEP 1

A   Draw a line down the length of the center of the paper.

B   Draw the proscenium opening. To do this you will need a scale ruler to measure the opening, or you can simply draw people lying head to toe across the proscenium. Again, this latter method allows you to proceed without bothering with scale and scale rulers. If you already have a scale floor plan, then using a scale rule is your best option. If you don't have such a plan yet, draw as many same-sized people as you need to determine the opening. This example has a 27′ opening, so it requires roughly 4½ people who are all 6′ tall.

C   Indicate the edge of the stage. In this example

it is 4′ from the proscenium — a little more than half a person.

D   Draw an edge of the set line on the floor plan. Draw another set line near the bottom of the paper. This will become the bottom of your set on the sketch.

E   Draw the floor plan of the set.

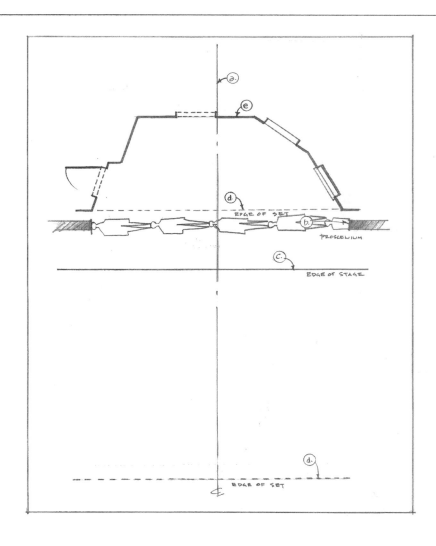

STEP 2

A   Starting at the centerline on the plan and moving offstage in both directions, mark 1″ increments along the set line. Label these marks in numerical order beginning with 0 at the centerline.

B   Draw vertical lines going upstage from each of these marks.

C   To complete the upper grid, mark off 1″ increments along the outermost vertical line. Mark these points in alphabetical order beginning with *A* at the set line.

D   Draw horizontal lines from each of these points across the set.

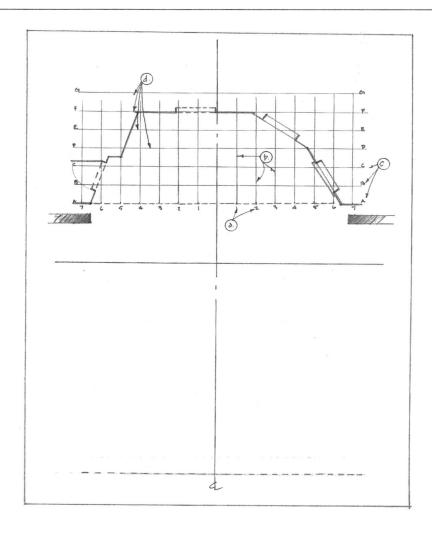

STEP 3

A   Draw a horizon line in the lower part of your sheet. This line is parallel to your set line and represents the eye level of someone in the center of the audience. You can determine the height of this line by examining a section drawing of the theater. You can also rough in its position by drawing it about 3′ to 6′ above the set line. In this example it's at 5′.

B   The intersection of the horizon line and the centerline is the center vanishing point (c.v.p.).

C   Establish an observation point (o.p.) along the centerline in the middle of the audience.

D   Draw lines from the o.p. to the marks that were lettered in step 2C.

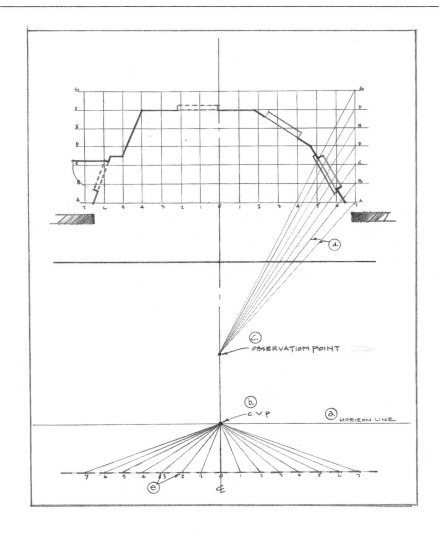

STEP 4

A   Mark the points where the o.p.A and the o.p.G intersect on the plan's set line.

B   Drop these points to the lower grid area. Draw vertical lines from each point to the outermost grid line in the lower grid.

C   Complete the lower grid by drawing horizontal lines from each point across the grid.

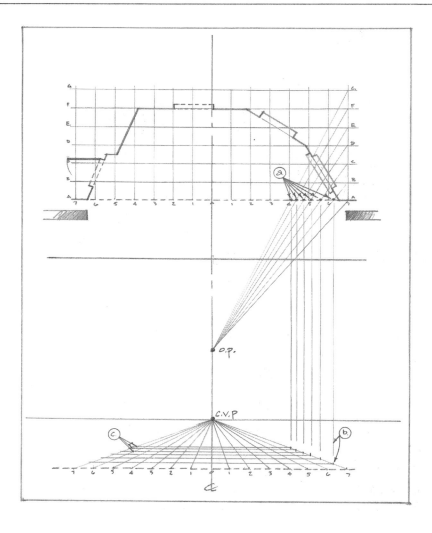

STEP 5

A   Draw the plan onto the lower grid by transferring the points where the set walls intersect onto the sketch. For example, in the plan the upper right corner of the set is at grid position *F4*. To draw this on the sketch, find grid position *F4* and make a mark. Do this with each set corner, and draw between your marks to complete the plan.

B   Draw vertical lines to represent the set walls. Begin these lines from the set corners and draw them to the middle of the page.

C   To draw the tops of the walls you will need to make a measuring stick. Mark 1'-scale increments along the most downstage stage right or stage left wall line. (Remember: If you aren't using a scale,

draw people the same size as the people in your plan.) In this case, the set is 12' high.

D   Establish the vanishing point for this wall by extending a line along the bottom of that wall to the horizon line.

E   From the 12' mark, draw a line to that same v.p.

F   Where this line intersects with the next vertical wall line is where the top of your wall ends.

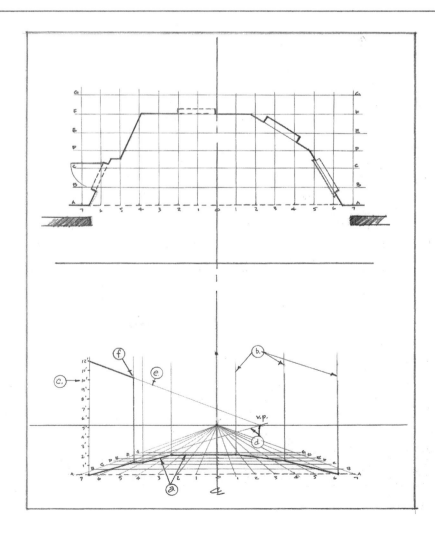

STEP 6

Establish the vanishing points for the other walls,
and draw the tops of the walls for the remainder of
the set.

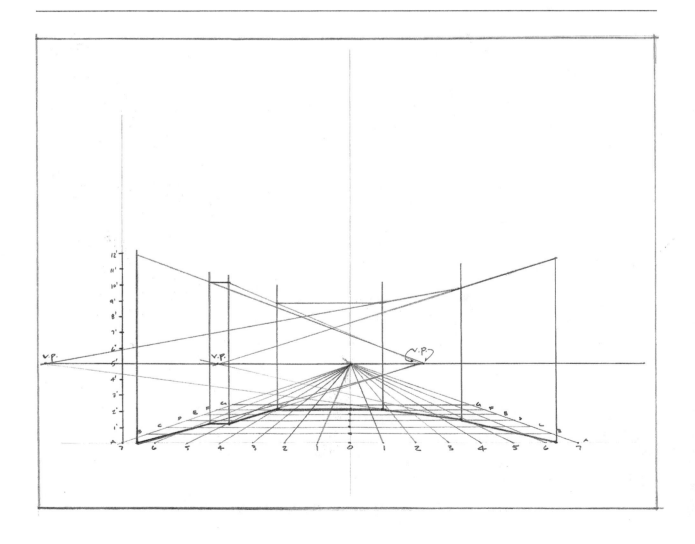

STEP 7

Establish the positions for the doors and windows by transferring them from the upper grid to the lower grid. Remember to measure the doors and windows with the measuring stick and transfer the items to the walls using each wall's vanishing points.

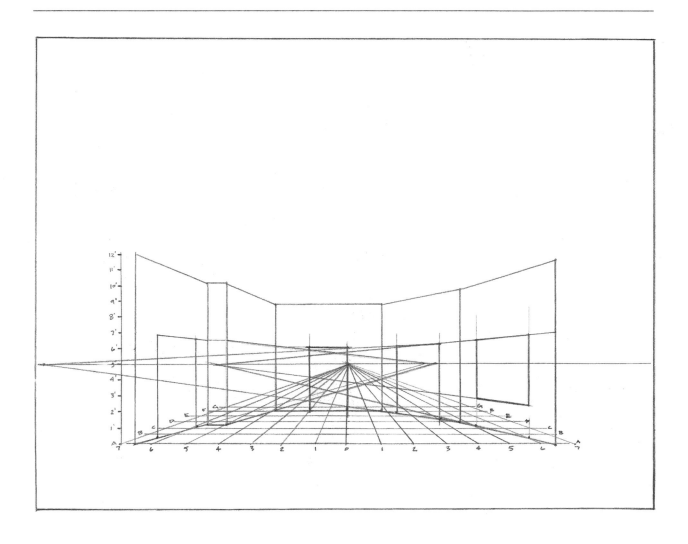

STEP 8

Transfer or trace the sketch to another sheet of paper.
Transfer only the set.

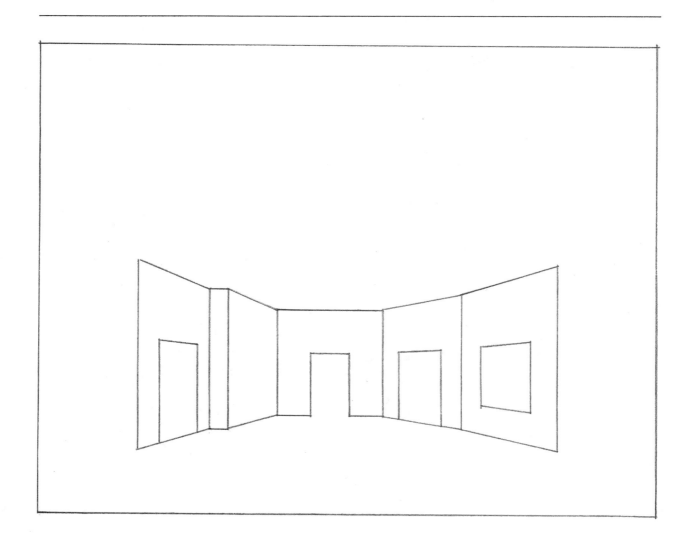

STEP 9

A Draw the set detail using the established vanishing points for each wall.

B (optional) Draw the proscenium and the edge of the stage.

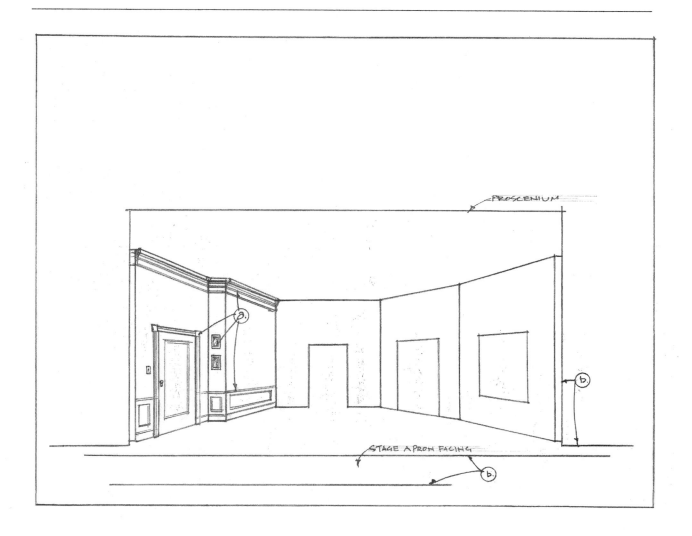

THE FINAL SET

Add the detail to complete the sketch. Note that most sample designs in this book do not include a person or furniture. This omission lets you see the set unobstructed. In your own final sketches, however, always include a figure and furniture.

6

Model Method

BUILD, THEN SKETCH

Perspective drawing techniques, even the simplified and modified ones presented earlier in this book, can be intimidating. I have found that some of my students shy away from *any* perspective techniques. For these students, I prescribe the procedure in this chapter—building a "model" of your set with found objects. You don't cut or glue anything. The model is only a stand-in that you will then draw on paper and transform into the actual design.

STEP 1

A Gather objects that approximate the shapes and sizes of the elements of your set design.

B Assemble the objects into a "model" of the set.

C Sit with your eye level below the middle front of the model. The model should be elevated — perhaps on a table. This means you will probably be sitting on the floor.

Model Method

STEP 2

Draw lines representing the edge of the stage and the back wall of the theater. Draw any theater architecture that may help you with your sketch. In this case, the proscenium was drawn. The purpose of these "guidelines" is twofold. One, they provide a boundary and a reference for the placement of your scenery. Two, if your sketches tend to look like they are drawn from the upper balcony, this step forces you to foreshorten. Not foreshortening enough results in those "as if drawn from the light-booth" sketches. If you know where the back of the theater is and make every attempt to keep the set downstage of it, the set is likely to "look right."

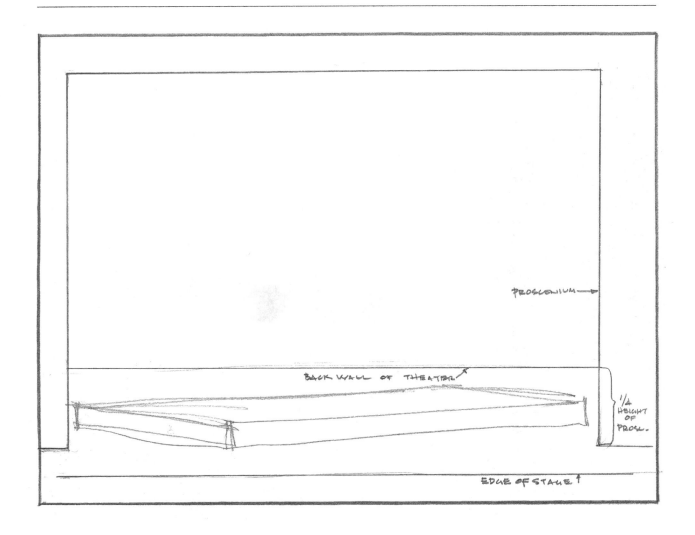

STEP 3

Rough in the shapes on your drawing paper. Don't be afraid of mistakes. You will most likely need to draw the shapes several times to place them correctly. Don't bother to erase any lines. Your cleaned up sketch will be transferred to another sheet of paper later on. Keep proportions accurate by measuring with a "drawing unit."

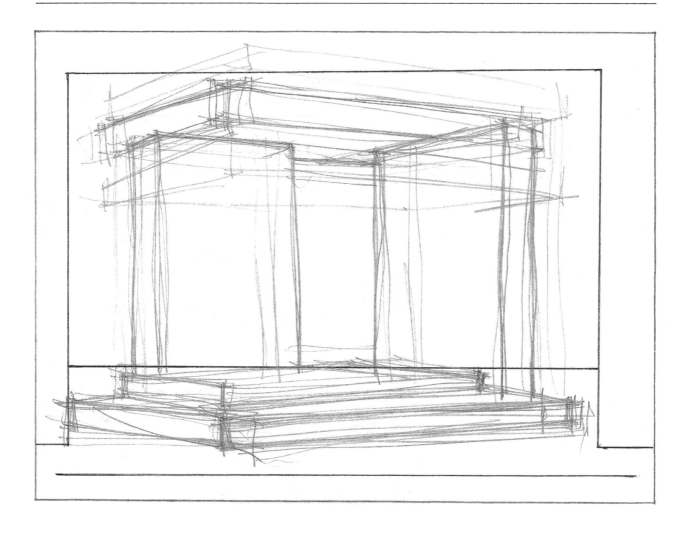

STEP 4

This step explains how to develop and use a drawing unit.

A Close one eye and while holding a pencil, extend your arm completely. Find a small, basic element that will become the drawing unit (in this case it's the height of the two books at the corner).

B Align the eraser with the top of the unit and your thumb with the bottom, marking that place on the pencil. This is your drawing unit.

C Measure elements in the model in units, and make sure the set elements on your *drawing* match up. After determining the unit on your model, you can downsize the unit in your actual drawing. The important thing is that proportions remain consistent.

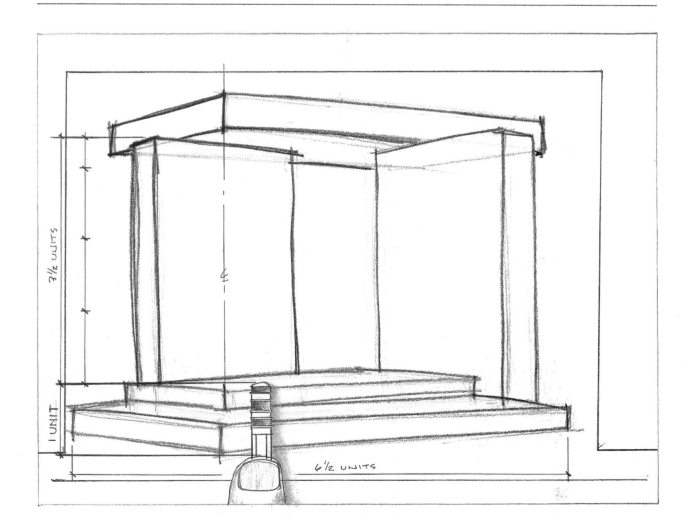

STEP 5

A   Check the relationships of elements to be certain they are positioned correctly. In this example, the corner of the top of the set and the steps below align with each other. These relationships must be congruous with the drawing.

B   Draw a horizon line. Remember that this is an approximation of your eye level.

C   Extend some of the set element lines out. You will notice that they don't line up at vanishing points.

D   Establish where you think vanishing points *should* be. This will be where most of the extended set lines seem to converge.

E   Correct the sketch by redrawing the set so the elements converge correctly at vanishing points.

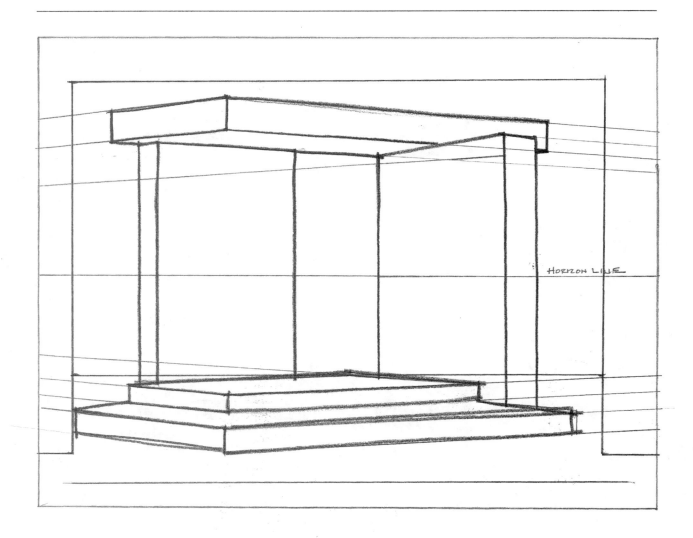

STEP 6
Transform your drawing into a set design. Add doors,
windows, steps, or whatever detail is required.

THE FINISHED SET

From videotapes to finished sketch, remember to
keep a consistently low eye level when sketching and
you won't go wrong. The shading around the perime-
ter of the set is discussed in a later chapter.

STEP 1

Let's look at another case study using this same technique. This time we'll combine some of the steps. Begin by assembling a model with found objects.

STEPS 2 AND 3

Sit in front of the model with your eye level below the middle of the model. The model should be elevated.

Draw in any of the theater architecture as a reference. Drawing the proscenium and back wall of the theater will provide a boundary and act as a reference for the placement of your scenery. This will force you to foreshorten, preventing those "as if drawn from the light-booth" sketches. If you know where the back of the theater is, and if you make every attempt to keep the set downstage of it, the set is likely to "look right." Rough in the shapes of the set pieces.

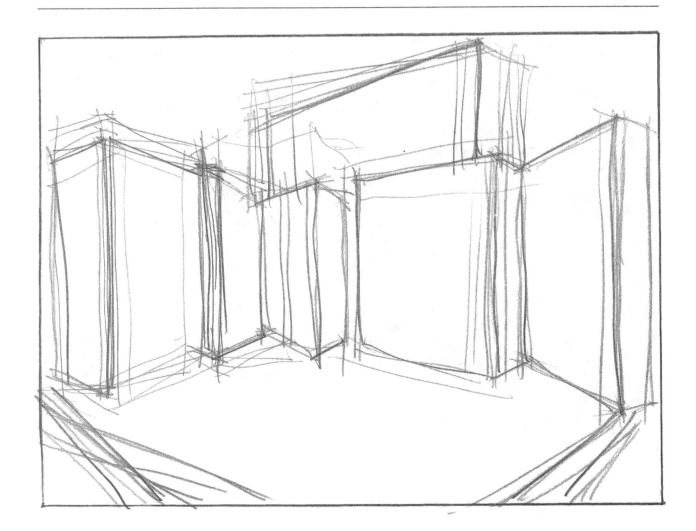

STEPS 4 AND 5

Develop your drawing unit — in this case, the width of the two center walls. Be sure to keep proportions consistent throughout. Check the relationships of elements to be certain they are positioned correctly. Draw the horizon line (an approximation of your eye level). Extend some of the set element lines out, and establish where you think vanishing points *should* be. Correct the sketch by redrawing the set so the elements in it converge correctly at vanishing points.

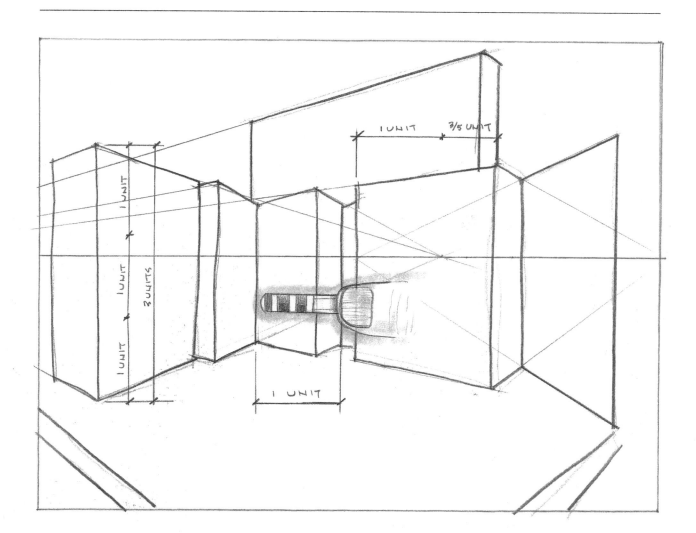

STEP 6
Begin adding the detail.

THE FINISHED SET

A grey felt marker was used for some of the toning
and shading in this sketch.

7

Thumbnail Method

DEVELOPING ON A SMALLER SCALE

If you can draw thumbnail sketches, this method might help you produce better sketches. For many people, filling up a large piece of paper is an overwhelming task. However, thumbnail sketching offers not only the possibility of eliminating these kinds of fears, but it can also be a terrific way to _develop_ the design. Since you don't have to fill a page to complete a design approach, you can produce many variations quite quickly. My students find this allows the drawing process to keep pace with the designing process.

STEP 1

Draw a thumbnail of your set. I find that drawing a
box provides me with a sense of the theatrical space.

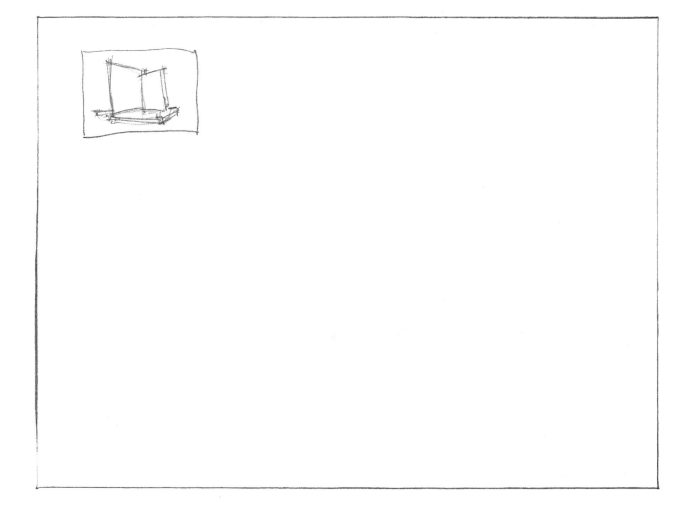

Drawing Scenery for Theater, Film and Television

STEP 2

Develop the basic design. Then fill the page with modifications of your design. None of these variations should take more than a minute or two to sketch.

STEP 3

Grid the design you would like to develop into a larger, more detailed sketch. It doesn't matter what units of measurement you use for the grid. Just be sure the vertical units and the horizontal units are the same length.

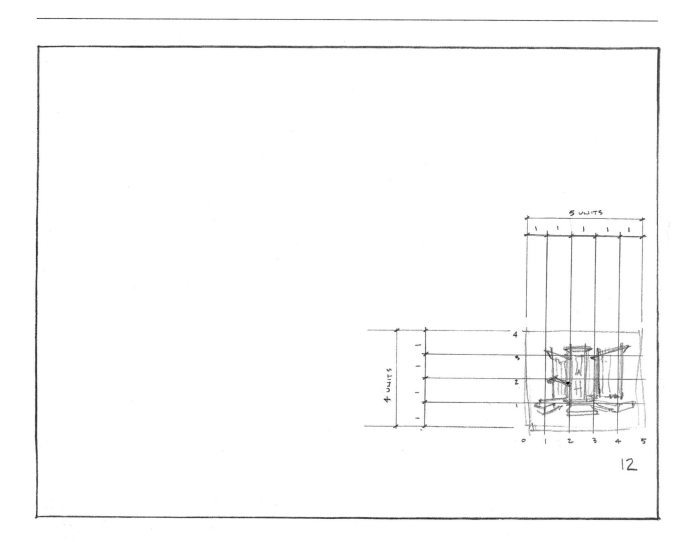

STEP 4

Using larger units, grid the sheet of paper that you
will develop the larger sketch on. (Again, the unit
size does not matter as long as the horizontal and
vertical sizes are equal to each other.)

STEP 5

Begin drawing *key* lines on the larger grid. Key lines will be the boundaries of each of the important scenic elements, if not *all* the elements. Take your time to do this carefully to ensure the proportions of the sketch match the thumbnail. Don't worry if the sketch looks a bit odd at this point. In subsequent steps you will adjust the set pieces so they "look right."

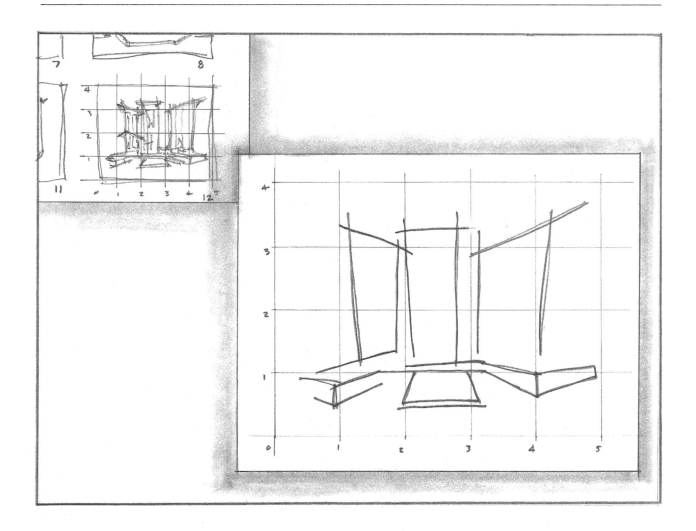

STEP 6

Examine each key line that you just transferred.
Correct the lines that need to be re-angled or reposi-
tioned. Don't erase the old lines. When you are
finished with the sketch, you can transfer it to
another sheet for a more finished look if you wish.

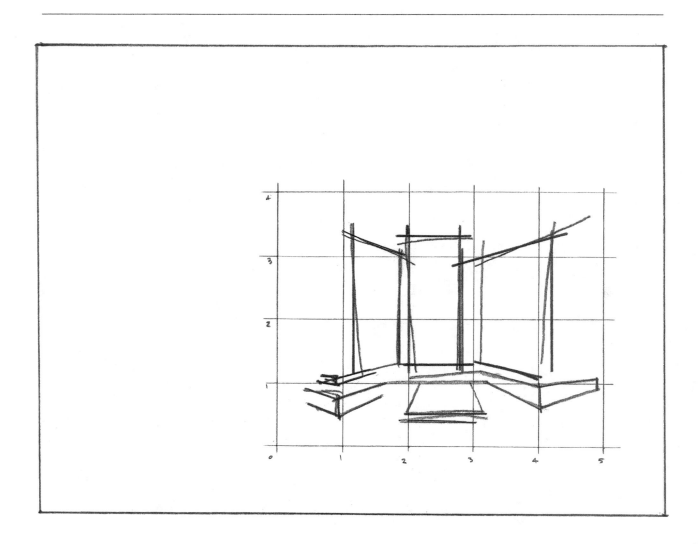

STEP 7

Fill in key missing lines and continue to correct
others. In this drawing, the "logic" of the platforms
needed to be developed. In other words, think about
how the various elements that comprise the set relate
to each other in terms of the physical space. Where
do the stairs end? Where does the wall meet the
platform? What line do you need to draw for the platform to have a fourth side? This is the step where
you must work on all issues of drawing logic.

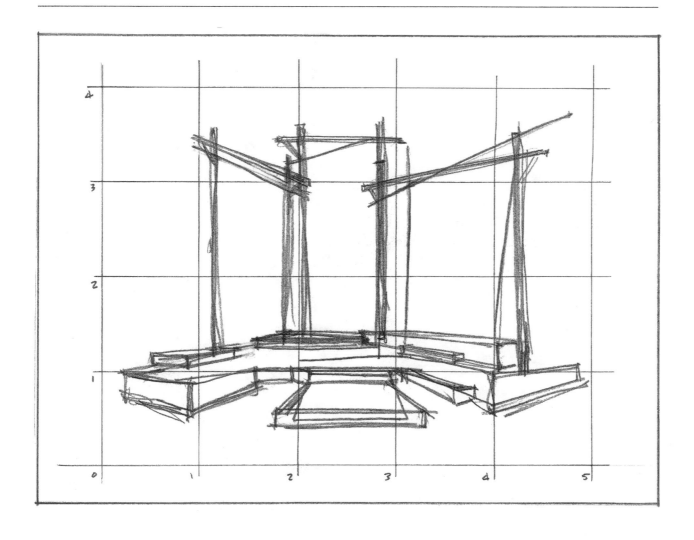

STEP 8

Begin adding larger detail. You may need to adjust
the set pieces for the detail to work correctly.

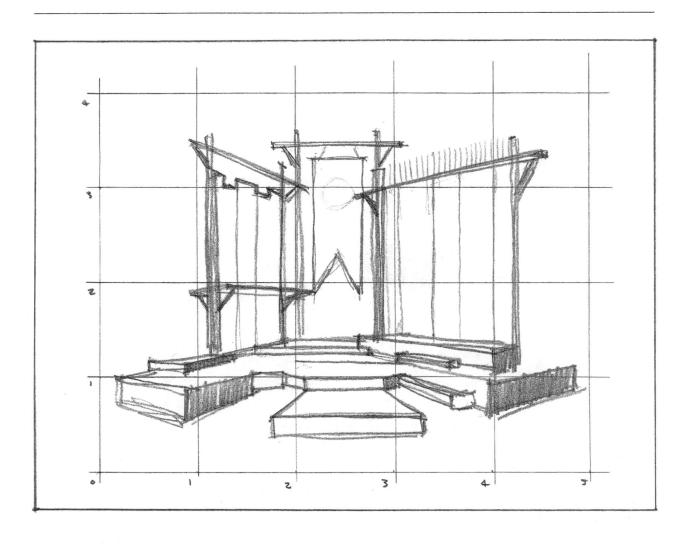

STEP 9

Add more detail. Your set should be taking shape by
now. Issues of logic, including perspective, should
all be resolved before adding too much more detail.

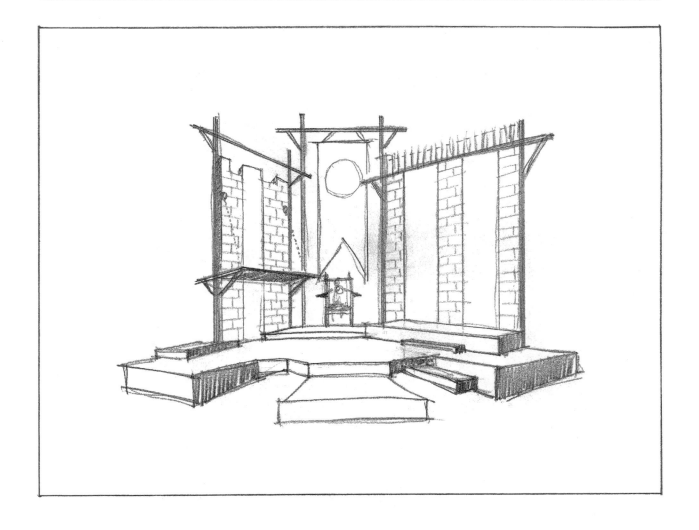

THE FINAL SKETCH

You may find that tracing paper lends itself to this technique. Instead of redrawing the same sketch to layer in the steps, you may want to add a layer of tracing paper for each step. This way you are simultaneously cleaning up and evolving the drawing.

8

Camera-View Method

FOR FILM OR TELEVISION

When it comes to developing a sketch for a film or television production design, the camera-view method is perhaps the most useful system in this book. If you want to know what the camera will see from a certain position on the soundstage (or on location), this is the method to use. This method is extremely accurate and in turn requires great accuracy on your part. Knowing some drafting techniques and being comfortable with a few drafting tools are both required for this approach. This technique is set apart from the other methods in this book because the sketch that results will be one as seen through the viewfinder. The technique is so specific to the camera that you must specify screen aspect ratio as well as the specific camera lens (in millimeters). For instance, varying these elements while keeping the camera position constant will yield quite different results.

Before you start, you will need some additional materials and information:

- **Screen aspect ratio** — The following example uses a wide-screen ratio of 1:1.85. This means that the screen image will be almost twice as wide as it is high. This will result in a 16″ wide by 8¾″-high drawing.
- **¼″-scale floor plan** — This is preferred because a ½″-scale floor plan will require larger paper and result in an almost 3′-wide drawing.
- **18″ × 24″ sheet of paper** — This will vary for different aspect ratios and different scales.

- **Tracing paper**
- **24″ straightedge**
- **Adjustable triangle**
- **T-square**
- **Scale rule**
- **Beam compass**
- **Colored pencils**
- **Camera lens (mm) / field-of-view chart** (Available from Larry Gordon Enterprises, 1430 Cahuenga Blvd., Hollywood, CA 90078, 213/466-3561)
- **Height of the set** — This example will have 10′-high walls.

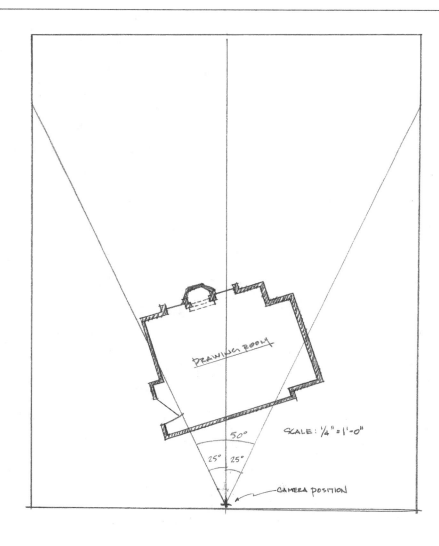

STEP 1 (LEFT)

Draw a centerline up the *very middle* of your tracing paper. Establish a camera position on the centerline at the bottom of your 18″×24″ tracing paper. Draw the field of view for your camera lens. Our camera lens yields a 50-degree angle. Carefully place the floor plan in the field of view. Make certain the camera "sees" exactly what you want the shot to contain and that it is placed at a realistic distance from the set (not outside the studio for example — you may need to use a wider lens). If this is a production design shot intended to show the whole set, like this example, then you will want to have a wide-angle lens or move the set away from the camera.

STEP 2 (BELOW)

Remove the "wild walls" from the drawing. Wild walls are walls that must be removed to shoot the interior of the set. Draw the horizon line. To do this, connect the points where the two field-of-view lines meet the edge of the paper. The horizon line should be parallel to the top of your sheet. If it isn't, check the accuracy of your field-of-view angles. Draw the curved picture plane. Use your beam compass to strike an arc that connects the two ends of the horizon line. The center of the radius is the camera position.

Next, draw ceiling and floor section lines on each side of the centerline. These lines must start at the front of the set and end at the back of the set. In this example they are 10′ apart since the set will be 10′ high.

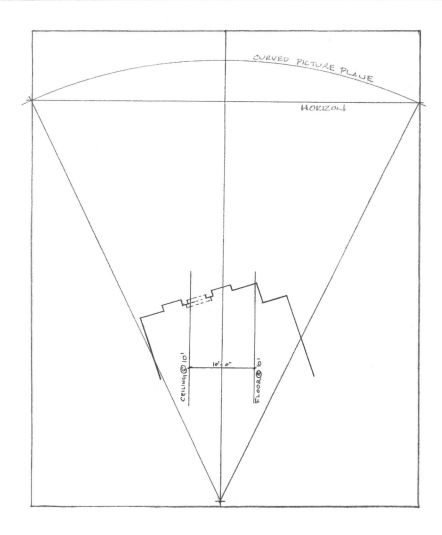

STEP 3

The camera-view method builds a sketch by establishing the corner lines of the set walls. This step establishes the first of the four corners necessary to draw this set.

Using the camera position as the radius, transfer corner 1 to the floor and ceiling lines in the plan. Draw an arc through corner 1 and through the floor and ceiling lines. Call the intersection of the arc and the floor and ceiling lines 1' (one prime).

Draw a line from the camera through 1' that intersects with the curved picture plane. Repeat this for the other 1'.

The distance between the two 1' marks on the curved picture plane (distance x) represents the height of corner 1. To draw corner 1 in the sketch, draw a floor line and a ceiling line equidistant (distance x) on either side of the horizon line.

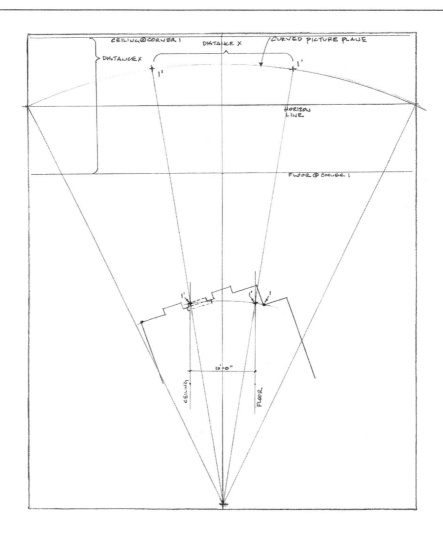

STEP 4

Draw a line from the camera through the actual corner 1 on the plan that intersects with the curved picture plane. This is the position of corner 1. Draw corner 1 through that point. Connect it with the corner 1 ceiling and floor lines.

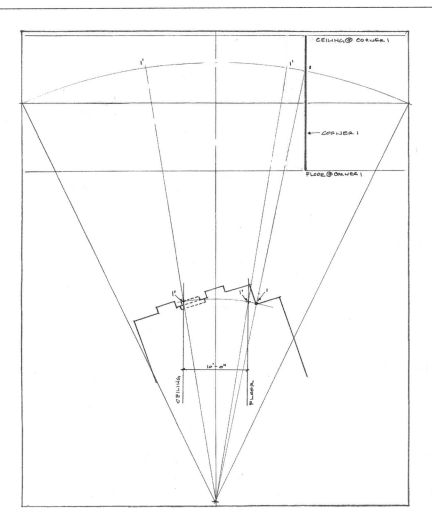

STEP 5

This step shows how to develop corner 2.

A Transfer corner 2 to the floor and ceiling lines in the plan. Draw an arc through corner 2 and through the floor and ceiling lines.

B Draw a line through 2′ that intersects with the curved picture plane. Repeat this for the other 2′.

C The distance between the two 2′ marks on the curved picture plane (distance y) represents the height of corner 2. To draw corner 2 in the sketch, draw a floor line and a ceiling line equidistant (distance y) on either side of the horizon line.

D Draw a line from the camera through actual corner 2 on the plan that intersects with the curved

picture plane. This is the position of corner 2. Draw corner 2 through that point. Connect it with the corner 2 ceiling and floor lines.

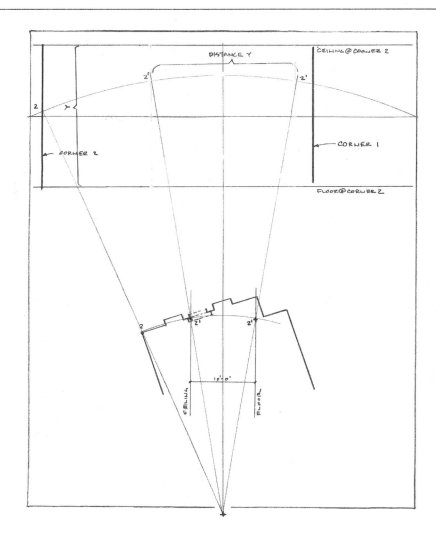

STEP 6

A Transfer corner 3 to the floor and ceiling lines in the plan. Draw an arc through corner 3 and through the floor and ceiling lines.

B Draw a line through 3′ that intersects with the curved picture plane. Repeat this for the other 3′.

C The distance between the two 3′ marks on the curved picture plane (distance z) represents the height of corner 3. To draw corner 3 in the sketch, draw a floor line and a ceiling line equidistant (distance z) on either side of the horizon line.

D Draw a line from the camera through actual corner 3 on the plan that intersects with the curved

picture plane. This is the position of corner 3. Draw corner 3 through that point. Connect it with the corner 3 ceiling and floor lines.

By connecting the tops and bottoms of corners 1 and 3, you can complete the wall. By continuing the top and bottom lines of this wall toward the horizon line, you can find one of two vanishing points in the sketch. This will come in handy for drawing in detail.

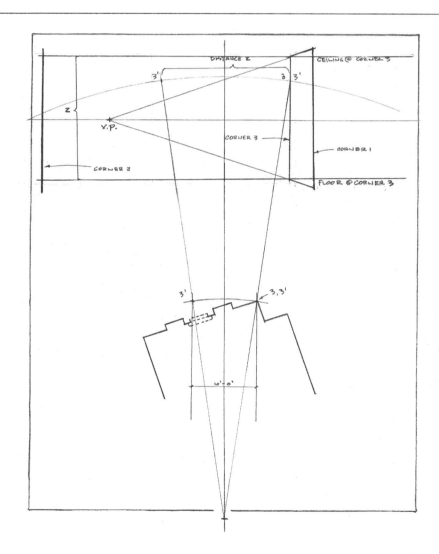

STEP 7

Draw corner 4 in the sketch by repeating the steps
outlined above.

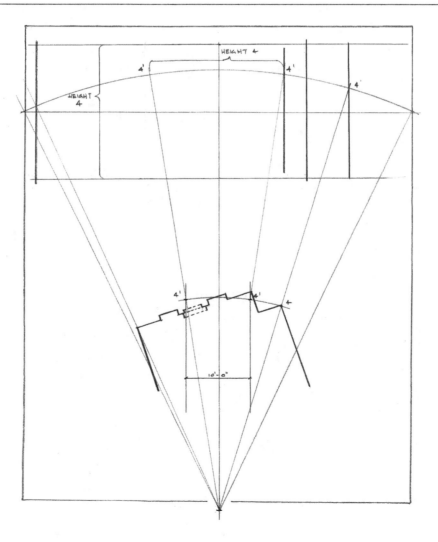

STEP 8

Connect the tops and bottoms of the wall corners to draw the walls of the set. If necessary, use the vanishing point to determine correct wall angles.

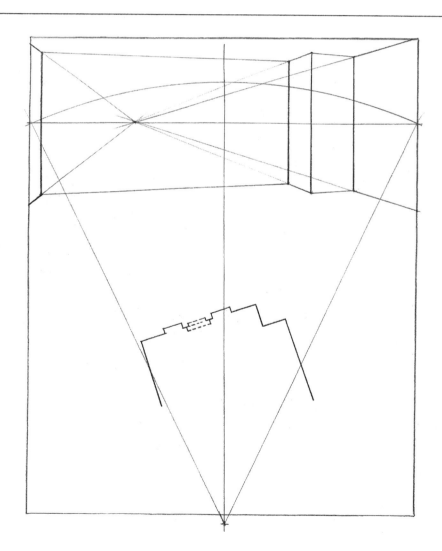

STEP 9

Begin drawing the detail. Transfer the positions of
important details to the curved picture plane.

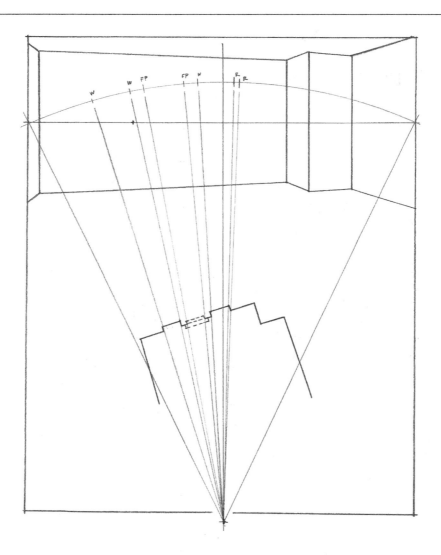

STEP 10

Draw vertical lines up and down from the curved
picture plane marks. These lines represent the horizontal boundaries of the detail.

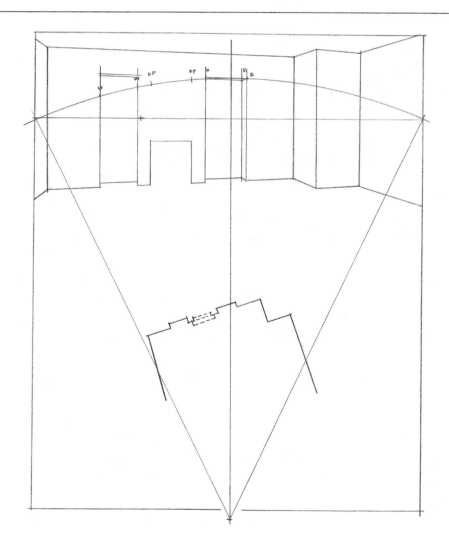

STEP 11

Complete the detail and the shading. The vertical position of the camera frame is your option. Remember that the distance between the top and bottom of the frame must coincide with the aspect ratio that results from your lens choice. In this example, the top and bottom of the frame are 8½" apart.

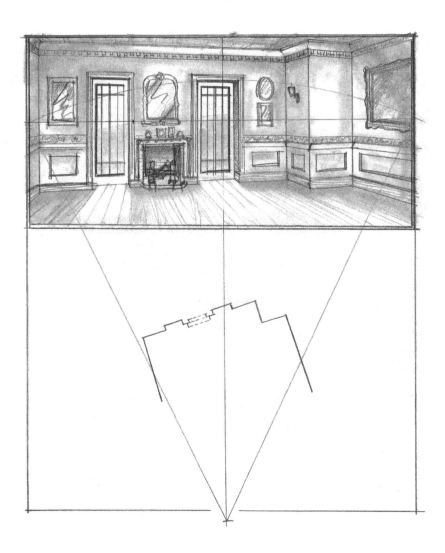

9

Variations — Without Walls

NONTRADITIONAL SETTINGS

If the set isn't a box set and the thumbnail or model methods aren't working as well as you would like, try going back to the modified-perspective methods in chapters four, five and eight. This may seem odd since the examples in those chapters were box sets. But this chapter explains how to modify those previously discussed methods to create a set without traditional walls, a set that is primarily platforms — there is no limit.

STEP 1

A   Establish phantom walls that are in line with the major set elements. This example develops the set that was sketched in chapter seven. That set consists of posts and panels (walls or banners). In the floor plan, phantom wall lines were drawn between pairs of posts.

B   Develop the phantom-walled version of the set using one of the modified-perspective techniques.

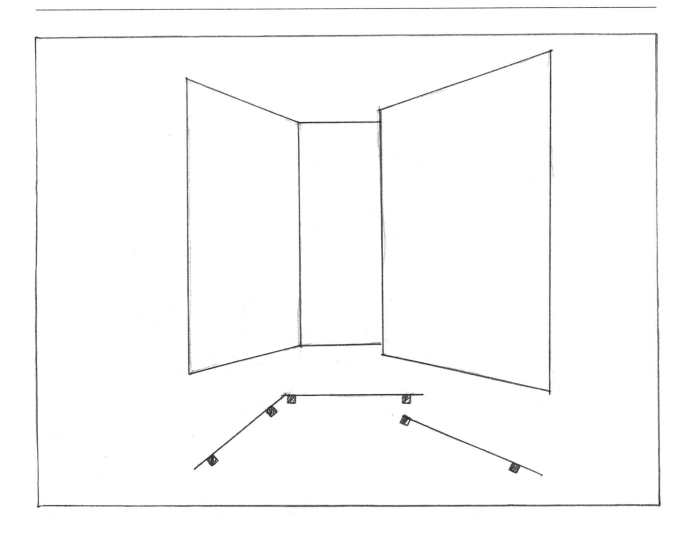

STEP 2

Draw the "nonwall" scenery that occupies the same space as the phantom walls in your perspective sketch. Use the phantom walls as a guide for overall height and width of the nonwall elements.

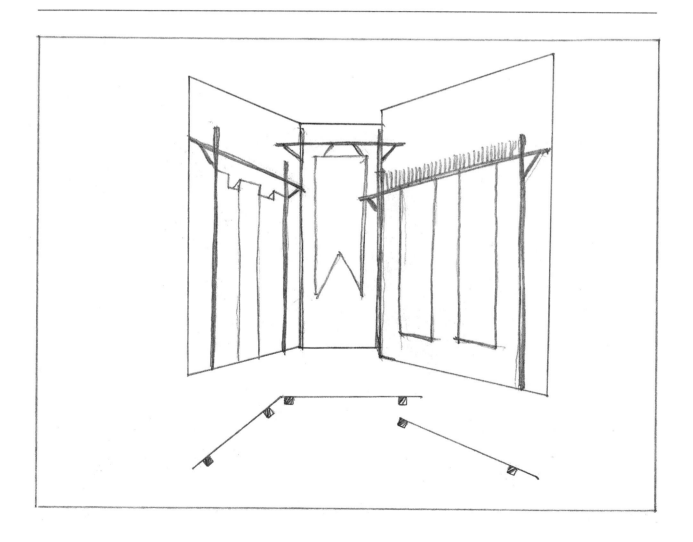

STEP 3
Complete the sketch.

STEP 1

In this variation, the floor plan consists of a set of platforms. There are two free-form walls behind the platforms. Phantom walls were drawn on the downstage edge of each platform. The phantom walls and the actual walls are then developed using one of the modified-perspective techniques. Detail is added and the sketch is completed.

In your floor plan, establish the phantom walls that will be replaced by nonwall scenic elements wherever they appear on your set. In this case you will develop a set made mainly of platforms with two free-form walls. In the floor plan, phantom wall lines were drawn at the fronts of platforms and at the free-form wall positions. Next, develop the phantom-walled version of the set using one of the modified-perspective techniques.

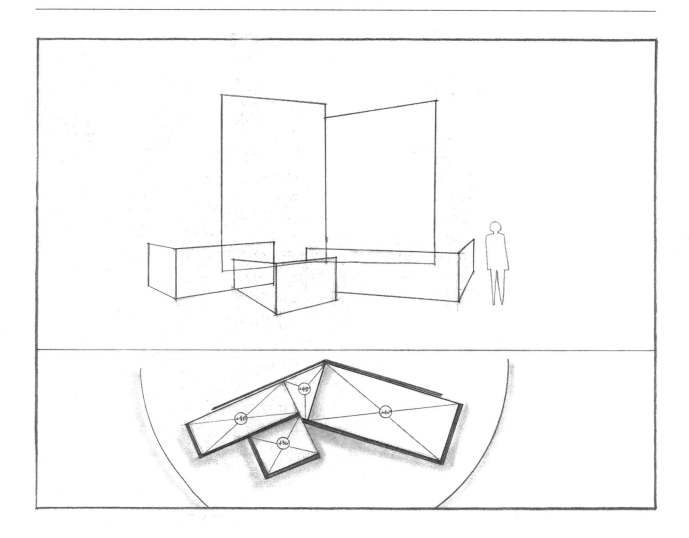

STEP 2

Draw the nonwalled platform front and back free-form walls that occupy the same space as the phantom walls in your perspective sketch. Use the phantom walls as a guide for overall height and width of the nonwall elements.

STEP 3
Complete the sketch.

10

Furnishings — Cubes to Couches

REALISM WITHOUT PERSPECTIVE

Most of the time it is easier to draw objects within the set without using *any* perspective techniques. Furniture and other items can be drawn with simple shapes such as cubes and cylinders or combinations of these shapes. You can then convert the shapes into chairs, couches and ferns. You can use perspective to achieve the same results, but it's quite time consuming. Practice transforming geometric objects into furniture in your sketch diary. Start by drawing simplified geometric shapes, then transform them into the finished product. Once this becomes second nature, your furniture will be quick and simple to draw; it will look less rigid, and your set sketches will look more fluid. Here are examples of simple geometric shapes turned into furnishings. You can copy these, vary them and use them as a guide in your designs. Simply adjust the orientation of the cube to match the perspective of the set in your actual sketch.

TABLES

Start with a simple cube. Add in the major elements
in simple "stick" form, first the legs and then the
top. Turn the "sticks" into filled-out legs. Add the
detail such as the overhang and the sides last.

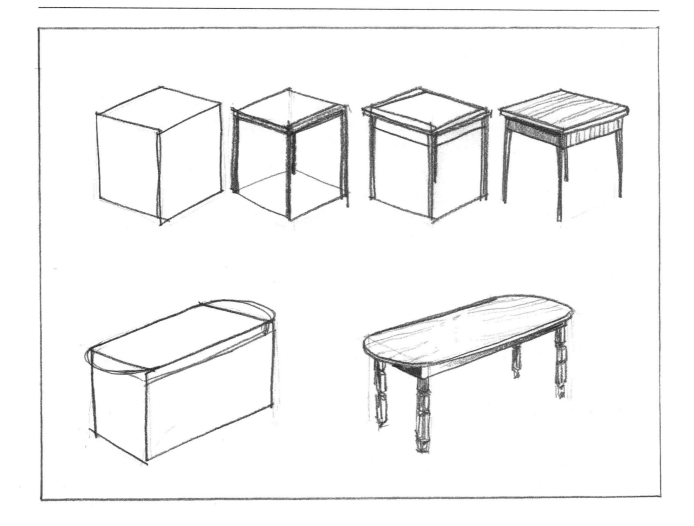

ROUND TABLE AND CHAIR

Notice that the ellipse of the round top touches each corner of the cube. The back of the chair is added as another rectangle (with perspective in mind). The back is bent and the legs are splayed for stability as they really are in chairs.

CHAIR AND LOVE SEAT

Here is a simple way of getting an upholstered look
by "carving" the cube. Notice that the shading helps
define the geometry.

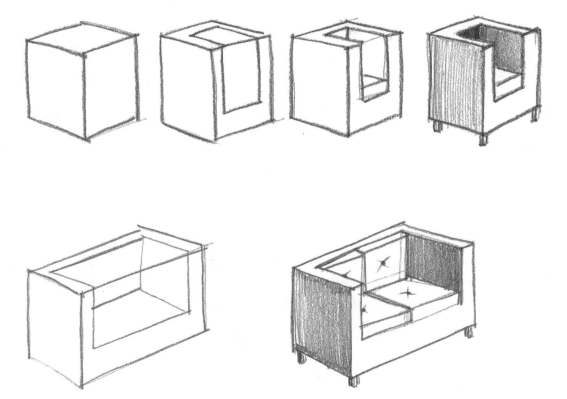

WING CHAIR AND COUCH

The chair and couch begin as the other high-back chair did. Next, simple shapes are added to occupy the positions of the winged sides, cushioned backs and armrests. The detail is added last.

DRESSER, REFRIGERATOR AND TOASTER

The dresser is essentially a table with sides. One of the sides has rectangles representing drawers. Even curved elements begin with a cube. The period refrigerator and toaster are sketched by curving two of the corners of the cube.

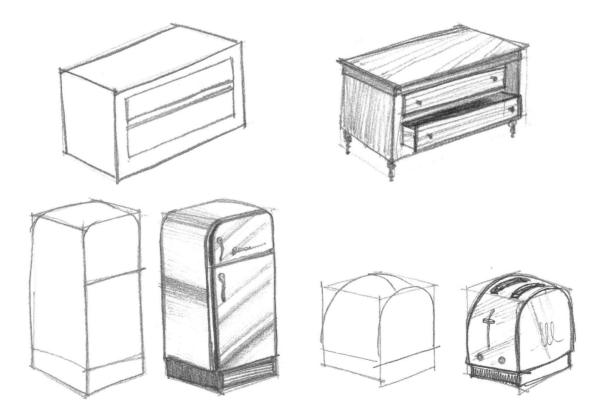

LAMPS

Both lamps start as cylinders and then are divided roughly in half with an ellipse. This represents the bottom of the shade. Smaller cylinders are drawn in the bottom half to become the lamp bases. The tapered, pleated shade consists of a smaller circle inside the larger one. The sides of the lamp are drawn from the middle circle to the smaller top circle to achieve the tapered shape. Alter the base by drawing the shape at the two outer edges of the lamp base cylinder.

STOVE AND TELEVISION

The back side of the cube for the stove is extended up slightly. Some slight curves are added for a period touch. The other details on the stove and television are drawn on the appropriate cube faces.

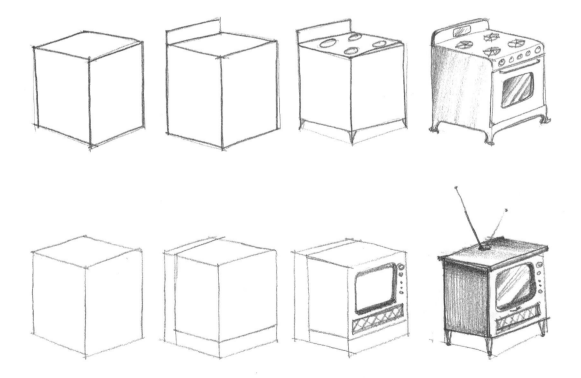

GRAND PIANO

The piano uses a double-width cube drawn on the top surface. It is repeated about a third of the way down to indicate depth. A shallow and narrow cube is added to the front for the keyboard. The top and legs are drawn last.

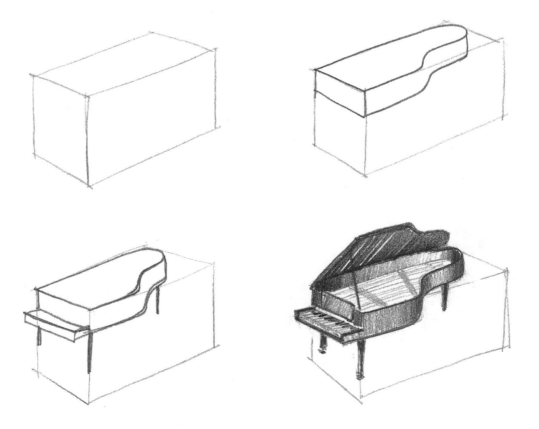

UPRIGHT PIANO AND STOOL

The shape of an upright piano is defined by its profile, which is drawn on the cube side. All the lines
of the profile are then drawn across the front of the
cube. Next, the profile is repeated on the other side
of the cube. Detail is added to complete the drawing.
The stool begins as a cylinder. The range of the top
and bottom elements is defined by drawing circles
concentric with the top and bottom of the cylinder.
These three shapes are then turned into the seat,
base and connecting post.

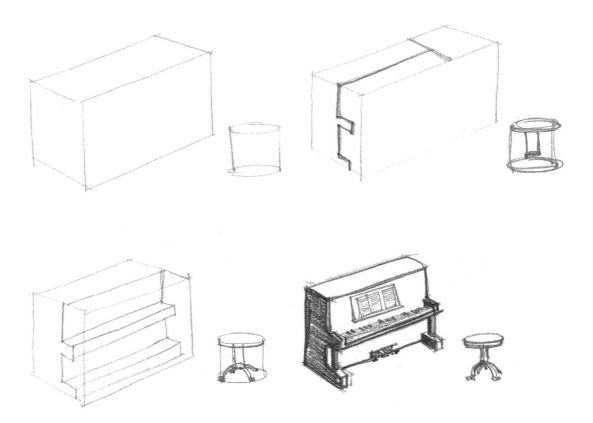

BED AND BREUER CHAIR

The bed's headboard and footboard are drawn on the appropriate cube faces. The mattress occupies about the middle third of two cube sides. The Breuer chair begins like all of the other chairs. The bent tubing, seat and back are defined by drawing at the cube boundaries, adding the curves where appropriate.

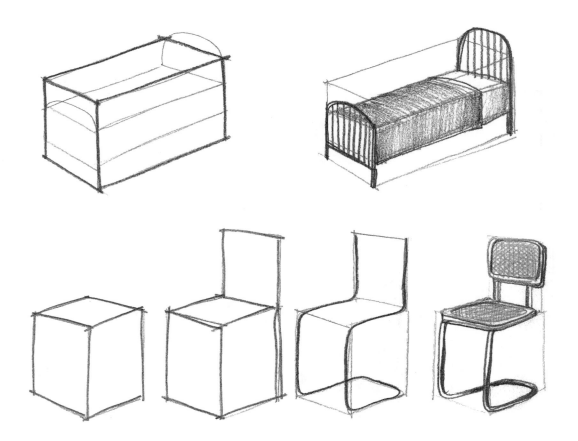

11

Textures and Surfaces

CONVINCING DETAIL

This chapter explores techniques for drawing textures, materials and some objects that can't be developed from cubes. It includes examples to meet almost any need. While many elements can't be born from the cube, the idea of creating complex shapes from simpler ones still applies. We'll look at a number of trees that you can easily develop from simple shapes that will lead you away from drawing "lollipop" trees. Textures add another layer to the drawing that can communicate so much about the character of the set. Whether it is a richly paneled room or a brick alley, these textures can add a great deal to the feeling of the sketch.

TREES

On the left is a generic palm tree. Without too much effort you can transform it into another size or variety. Start with the rectangle of the base and then add the circle that represents the growth boundary. A few lines for branches are all you need to complete the planning phase. Zigzag variations are used to draw the trunk and leaves.

On the right is a small tree. Again, the planning phase consists of quickly drawn, simple shapes. Random squiggles filled in with a stomp complete the sketch.

BANANA TREE

The banana tree begins with a skeleton representing the trunk. The leaves are drawn on the skeleton. Inside folds are filled in, and lines are drawn representing the striations of each leaf. The drawing is finished by applying random stomp strokes.

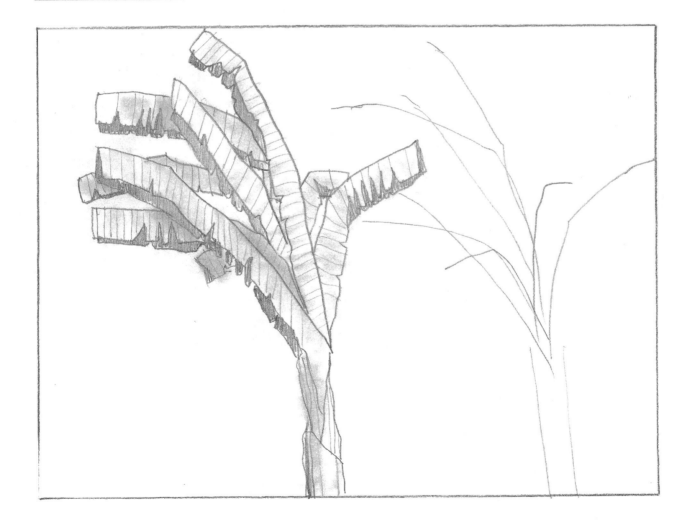

PINE TREE

The pine tree begins with a triangle on a short rectangle. The shape is filled with zigzag strokes. The tree is finished by drawing short needle strokes on the edge of the tree.

MORE TREES

In this sketch for the *Oklahoma!* dream ballet, a felt
pen was used to draw in simple, single-stroke trees.

EXTERIOR SURFACES

A To render glass, draw diagonal guidelines on the window. Start very dark in the upper left corner and fade to the white of the paper. Use pencil and stomp strokes to complete the job.

B To draw shingles, start with two horizontal guidelines. Then add vertical lines of random widths between the guidelines. Connect the vertical lines with short horizontals of varying heights. The result is a random shingle effect for walls or roofs.

C For bricks, sketch in both horizontal and vertical guidelines. Draw double horizontal and vertical lines over your guidelines, staggering the verticals if you want. Fill in random bricks with a mid-tone grey and a darker grey. Leave about a third of the bricks white.

D The description that follows can apply to paneling, flooring or even single posts or beams. For a realistic-looking wood, draw the grain lines in pairs. Look closely at this example and you will see that all of the grain is paired off. Vary the pattern in each board, plank or beam. Try a long pattern where the grain lines go from edge to edge. Always carry a grain line to the edge of the board; never allow grain lines to stop midway on the board.

GLASS SHINGLES

BRICK WOOD

EXTERIOR EXAMPLES

This example contains variations on wood clapboard,
brick and shingles.

MORE EXTERIOR EXAMPLES

An example of brick and concrete paving.

WALL SURFACES

A The stucco and concrete textures are achieved by tapping the drawing with the tip of a handful of lead pencils. The concrete variation is accomplished by drawing curved lines for pits and by mottling the surface with a stomp for variation in color.

B Drawing vein guidelines is the first step in achieving a marble look. The next step is to draw jagged lines that loosely follow the guidelines. The stomp is then used to draw discoloration that roughly follows the vein lines. The last step is to draw short, dark, random vein lines.

C The first step in drawing block is to draw the guidelines. The block can then be finished using the marble or stucco method. It is important with block to draw double lines that represent the mortar.

D Wallpaper can be indicated with the sketchiest of detail. The important thing is that wallpaper looks like wallpaper and not like cracks or some other form of wall decomposition. The key to success is the geometry. In this example a ribbon-and-bow design is placed on a grid. Without a geometric guide the pattern gets lost and won't appear to be wallpaper.

WALLPAPER

In this sketch a simple wavy line indicates Victorian wallpaper. It appears as paper because of the geometry and not the pattern.

MORE WALLPAPER
The rose wallpaper in this sketch relies on the geometry to tell the story.

EXTERIOR VARIATIONS
A variation on brick and concrete.

MIRRORS, CURTAINS

A   For mirrors and other reflective materials you use a technique similar to creating windows. This time little if any stomp work is used.

B   For sheer curtains you use a simple technique with a big payoff. At the bottom of the curtain, draw a simple, slightly curved line with short, unconnected strokes. Using a straightedge, draw random vertical lines. Without the straightedge, draw very narrow, inverted *V*s from the top of the drape. Finally, fill in the curtains with random stomp strokes.

C   For other curtains draw a curved line for the bottom of each curtain. Draw vertical lines up the edges of each curve. Use a stomp or pencil to shade each fold where the material goes back.

REFLECTIVE

SHEER OR THIN CURTAIN

FINAL SKETCH

This sketch shows examples of both sheer curtains
and reflective Mylar strips.

WOOD FLOORING

Here are two examples of wood flooring. The finished
wood is distinguished from the rough wood using
longer, narrower boards and a lighter and simpler
grain. The reflection was created by erasing sections
of the drawing and leaving out knots and nails.

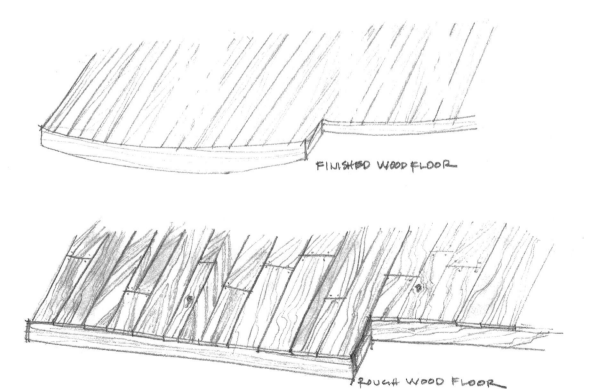

FINISHED WOOD FLOOR

ROUGH WOOD FLOOR

Drawing Scenery for Theater, Film and Television

TILE

This exterior tile is simple to create and is highly believable. After gridding out the floor, grass and leaves are added. Stomp work at the upper left corner of each tile gives the sense of a slightly curved surface. Bigger stomp swaths give the sense of shadowed and discolored areas.

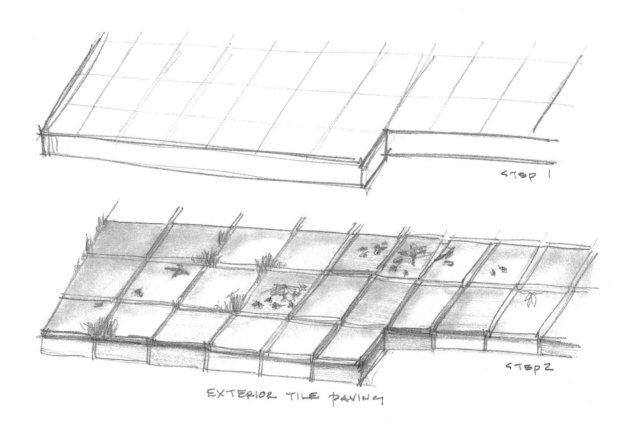

STEP 1

STEP 2

EXTERIOR TILE PAVING

FINAL SKETCH
A final sketch with tile paving.

HUMAN FIGURES

Adding human figures to a drawing is a must. It gives the viewer a sense of size and scale. Here are two methods for drawing a simple figure.

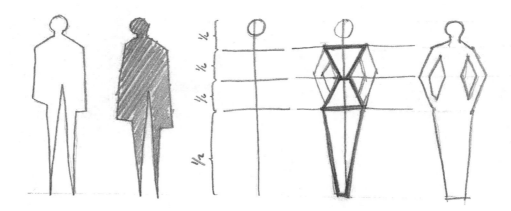

12

Shading, Toning and Atmosphere

THREE-DIMENSIONAL MOOD

The finishing touch for your sketch is shading and toning. A skillfully shaded sketch can capture a mood and convey the atmosphere of a particular moment in the play. Shading will also make your set appear three-dimensional. After establishing a light source, you will then tone the shaded sides of objects and scenery and indicate shadows. Here are some important shading and toning rules covered in this chapter: 1. Shadows "converge" at the light source. 2. Tonality must define shape as much as lines do. 3. When two planes meet, there must be a tonality difference. 4. Checkerboarding separates architectural surfaces. 5. Walls should gradate dark to light from top to bottom. 6. Tonal contrast lessens as you go upstage or farther away from the "front" of the sketch. By mastering these shading and toning rules, you can light the set to fit the mood of the play.

BEFORE — WITHOUT SHADING
A sketch waiting for detail and shading to be applied.

AFTER—WITH SHADING
With atmosphere and detail.

STOMP WORK (BELOW)

The stomp shading tool is useful for creating shadows and tone. The two strips rendered here show tonal gradation. Both were sketched with a drawing pencil and were originally identical to each other. The bottom strip was then "smudged" with a stomp. This resulted in a more blended gradation and a softer appearance; the individual pencil strokes are obliterated leaving only the nuance of tone.

LIGHT SOURCE (RIGHT)

The lightbulb on the far right represents a light source. The five cubes show the light's effect in terms of shadow and shading.

A The *a* cube is a schematic that shows the logic of the shading. The light source is high (above the top of the cube). The top face is the only one with direct light. This surface will remain the lightest in value with no tone at all. The surface that points away from the source is shaded the darkest. The medium surface gets *some* light from the source.

B The *b* cube shows the result of the shading described above.

WITHOUT STOMP

WITH STOMP

C   The *c* cube has an added shadow. The "top" of the shadow is about parallel to the top of the cube. The angle of the shadow follows the rules of perspective. If you trace the two sides of the shadow and extend those lines back, they converge at the lightbulb. A grounding line—the thin blurry line at the bottom of the cube—was also added here. It is drawn with the stomp (and sometimes a straightedge). Its purpose is to make the cube seem anchored to the surface rather than floating. An important rule of toning says that where two planes come together, you must slightly alter the tone of one of them so they look like they are coming into contact.

D   The *d* cube shows the effect of the stomp over the pencil shading.

E   Shading must define the dimensionality of walls, furniture and other objects in your sketch as much as lines do. Cube *e* shows that a shape can be defined with tone alone, just as cube *a* does so with lines alone.

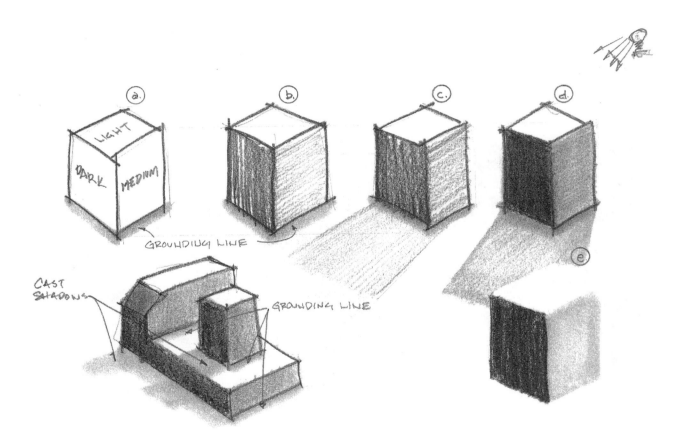

SHADING FURNITURE

The effects of shading on some cube-based furniture.

NONLINEAR SHADING

Stomp shading was used here to create nonlinear dimensionality. The spheres began as circles. The column began as a rectangle. The drapery folds were shaded as if they were half columns.

CORNER SHADING

This corner detail of a box set has just begun to be shaded. You can see that wherever different planes come together, a grounding line is drawn with the stomp. This technique anchors the planes to each other and shows that one plane is in back of a primary plane.

TONING WALLS

These walls were toned in the following manner:

A   Wall 1 is toned darker where the two come together. Notice the arrows indicating the direction of gradation (from dark to medium to light). The wall lightens as you move offstage.

B   Similarly, the bottom of the staircase wall is also darkened. Walls that face stage right will be toned darker than those facing stage left.

C   Look along the top of the set. At the points where the four surfaces meet, they alternate between light and dark. This *checkerboarding* allows you to define the dimensions of the architectural surfaces.

D   The top third of the set should be toned darker than the bottom two-thirds.

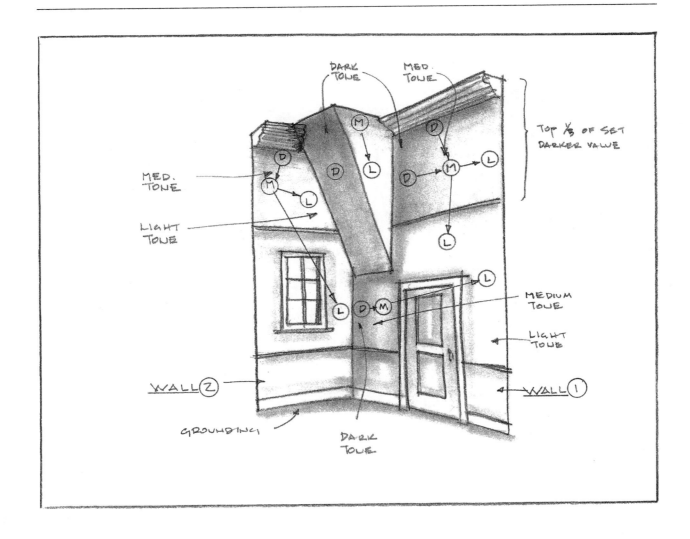

FINAL SHADING

This drawing illustrates the last steps in your sketch.

A Darken any offstage elements that will be quite dark or unlit during the show. Grade from darkest at the top to lightest at the bottom.

B Using your stomp, shade out the upper extreme corners of the set. These places will be the darkest and should look that way in the rendering.

C The room in the distance was wiped once with the stomp to give it uniform tonality. Lowering the contrast for distant objects is another important rule to remember. In this case, you could give that back room more contrast with interesting shading. But remember that the degree of contrast must be lower — lighter darks and darker lights — than the rest of the sketch.

D Note that for more dramatic productions shading will be darker and more heavy-handed. Be appropriately subtle and use a light touch for musicals and comedies.

STOMP
DARKENED
CORNERS

BACKGROUND
IS DARKENED
TO ONE
TONE

FOUND A PEANUT
A sketch made more dramatic with shading.

13

Transferring the Sketch

PREPARING FOR RENDERING

Now that your sketch is complete it's time to prepare for the rendering. The rendering is typically used in addition to or in place of a scale-color model. It can also be used with a color model to show other scenes in a multi-set show. Typical set rendering media include gouache, dry or tube watercolor and felt marker. While this chapter doesn't actually go through the process of applying the color, it does investigate two methods of transferring the sketch to the rendering surface. The rendering material is usually watercolor paper, felt marker paper or illustration board.

FIXATIVE

To prevent smudging it's a good idea to apply fixative
to your sketch. You can buy fixative in any art supply
store. It comes in a spray can and is easy to apply.

TRANSFERRING THE SKETCH TO WATERCOLOR PAPER

STEP 1

Tape a sheet of watercolor paper to your work surface. Tape a sheet of graphite paper on top of that. (Don't use carbon paper; it resists watercolor.) Make sure the graphite faces down and contacts the watercolor paper. (If you are desperate, you can make your own graphite paper by scribbling heavily on a sheet of paper.)

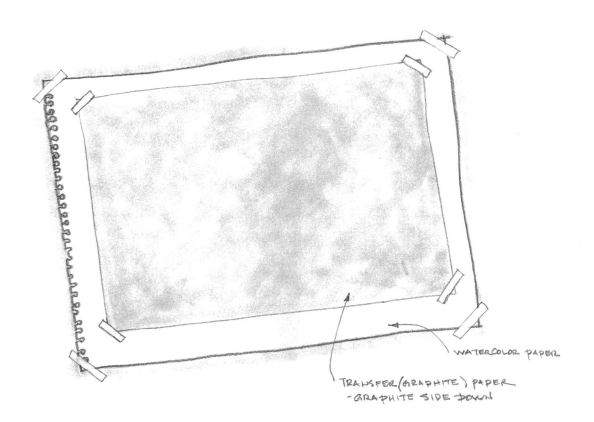

WATERCOLOR PAPER

TRANSFER (GRAPHITE) PAPER
- GRAPHITE SIDE DOWN

STEP 2

Tape the sketch — or better yet a photocopy of the
sketch — on top of the graphite paper "sandwich."

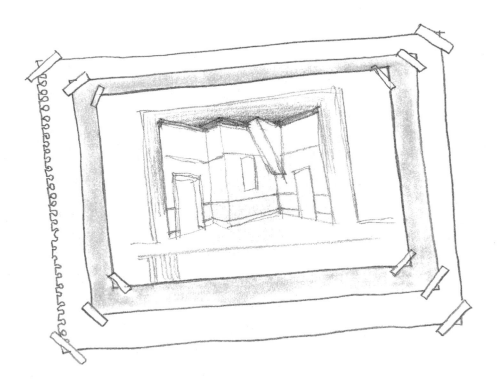

STEP 3

Begin the transfer process by drawing over the lines on the sketch. Since this will ruin the sketch, you may want to use the photocopy. Using a colored pen will let you know instantly which lines still need to be traced.

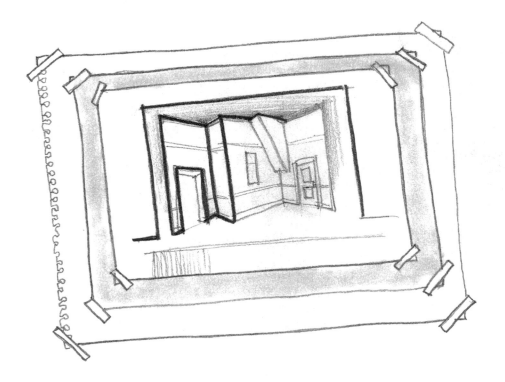

STEP 4

Remove the graphite paper to reveal the transferred sketch.

TRANSFERRING THE SKETCH TO MARKER PAPER

STEP 1

Tape your original sketch to a work surface.

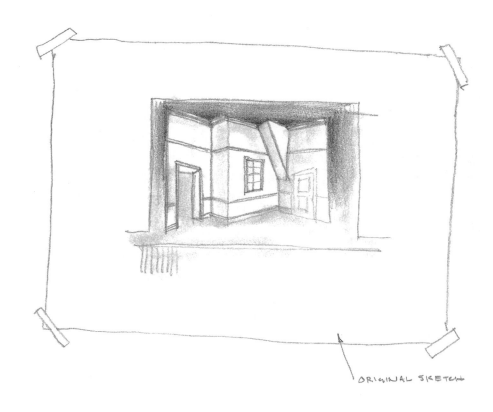

ORIGINAL SKETCH

STEP 2

Tape marker paper over the sketch. Marker paper is
translucent enough to allow the sketch to show
through.

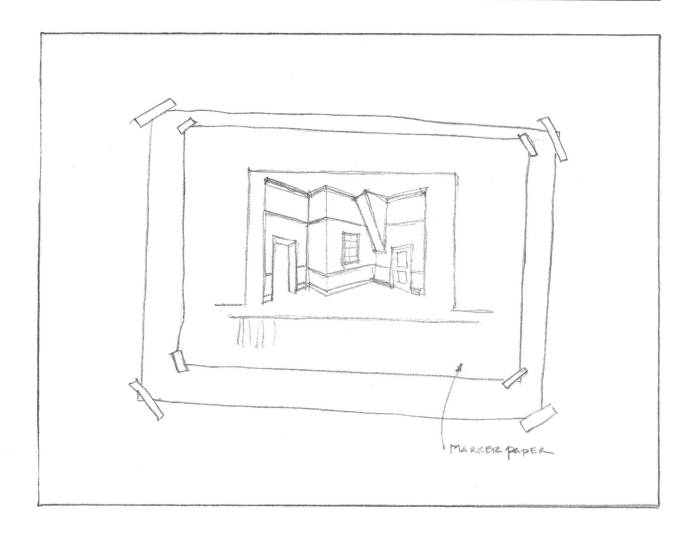

MARKER PAPER

STEP 3

Trace the sketch onto the marker paper. Use either
pencil or pen. If you are using pen, make certain the
ink is waterproof and your markers won't dissolve it.

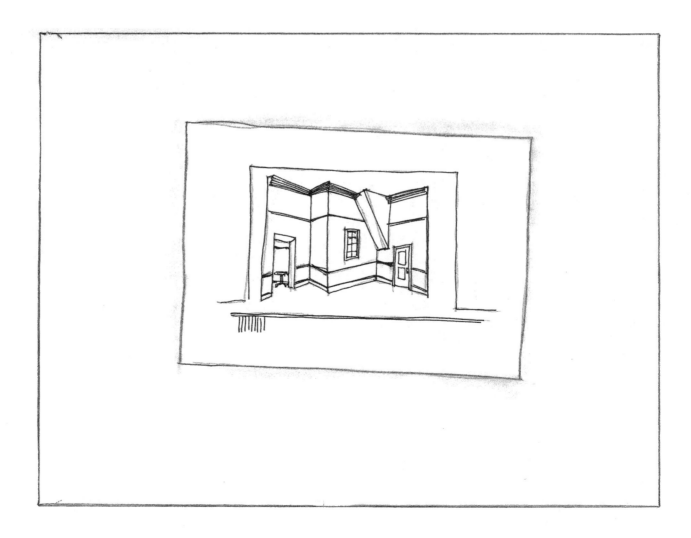

STEP 4

Lay in several values of grey marker to complete a
black-and-white sketch or the first phase of a color-
marker rendering.

14

Matting

PRESENTATION

Framing the sketch with a matt is a very simple way of improving the presentation of your design. This chapter presents a quick method for determining the best size matt for your sketch. Black-and-white sketches look best in a black matt. The high contrast of the black matt creates a better frame for your sketch. It pulls the viewer's eye inward to the sketch. A black matt is also a closer approximation of the darkened theater space around the staging area. Grey and white matts are less preferred options.

STEP 1

Place the sketch on a large work surface. Take one page of a newspaper and decide on the best position for the bottom opening of the matt. Play around with different options before settling on a solution.

STEP 2

Position another sheet of newspaper at the top of the
sketch to determine the top opening for the matt.

STEP 3

Use two more sheets of newspaper to determine the
two side openings. Again, play around with all the
newspaper sheets until you achieve the perfect look.
Tape the sheets together—not to the sketch.

STEP 4

Remove the newspaper from the sketch and position it on the reverse side of a sheet of matt board near a corner. In this example, the opening is 2″ from the lower left side of the board and 2½″ to 3″ from the bottom of the board. Trace the opening onto the matt board. Don't worry about straight lines. Draw freehand, keeping close to the newspaper opening.

STEP 5
Remove the newspaper and correct your lines.

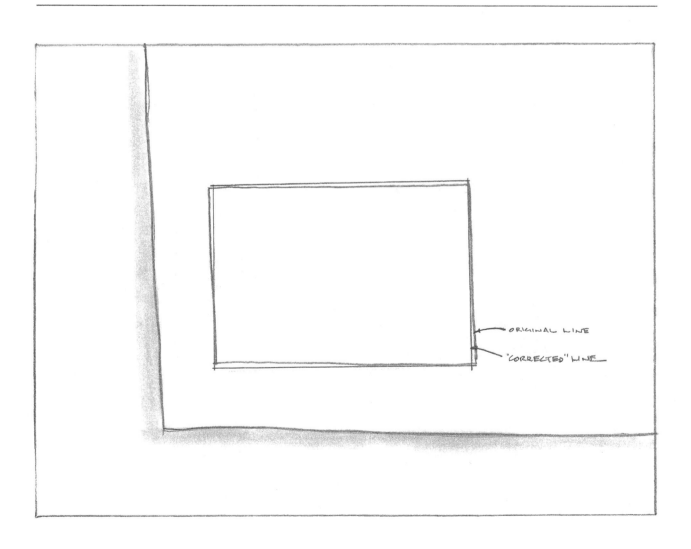

STEP 6

Draw the other two lines for the other sides of the
matt. In this example, the top and side lines are 2″
away from the opening. Why is the bottom line more
than 2″? An optical illusion is at work here. If the
bottom border were 2″, the visual weight of the picture "bearing down" would actually make the bottom
border look smaller than 2″. You must compensate
by making the bottom border a bit wider.

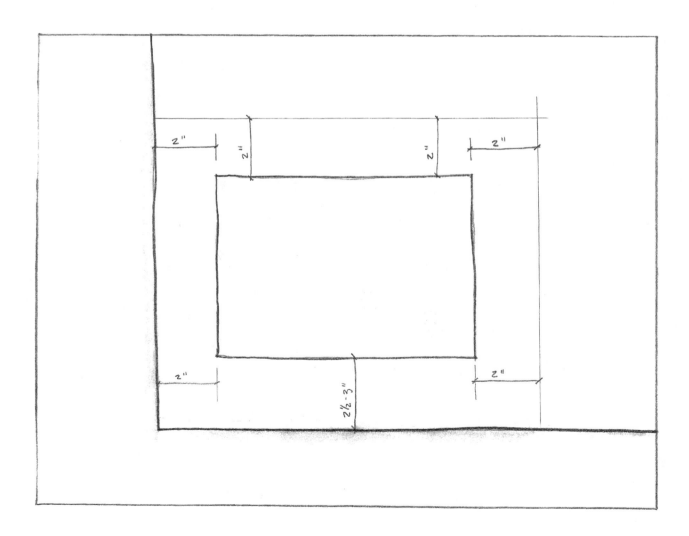

STEP 7

A Place the matt board on a soft cutting surface. This will keep the blade sharp and prevent the knife from slipping so easily.

B If you are right handed, place a metal-edged ruler on the left side of the line to be cut.

C Hold the ruler with your left hand and cut down, or to the right, with your right hand. Reverse these instructions if you are left handed. Always keep your hand at the top of the cut. This way, if the knife slips, your hand won't be in the way.

D To make the cut, use four or five *light* strokes. If you use lots of pressure, the knife may slip and cut deep into whatever is in the way.

E Always use a sharp new blade and have a pack of new blades ready. If you can't cut through after four or five gentle passes with the knife, it's time to change the blade.

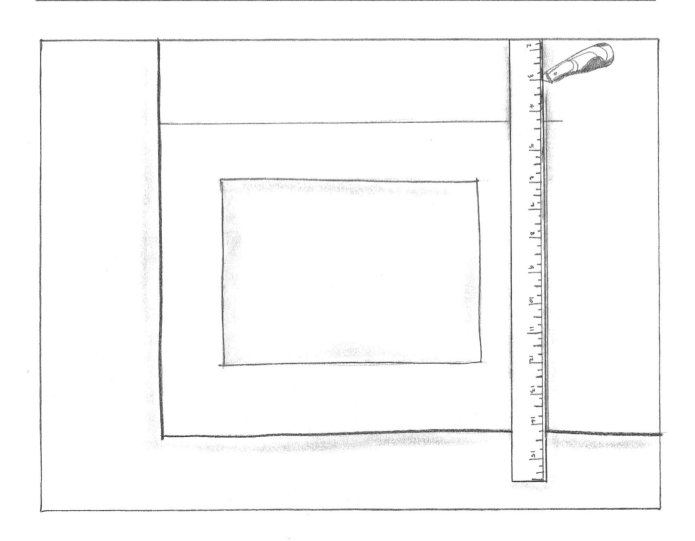

STEP 8

More elaborate or decorative matt cuts can be made
by cutting at a 45-degree angle and achieving a bevel
cut. This takes quite a bit of practice, and matt-
cutting machines make this easier to accomplish.
Another simple way to get a more intricate look is to
cut away the thin, black outer paper of the matt board
at the opening. In this example, a score (one or two
light passes with the knife) was made about ¼″ away
from the opening in the matt all the way around. The
colored paper layer is then peeled quite easily from
the cardboard backing.

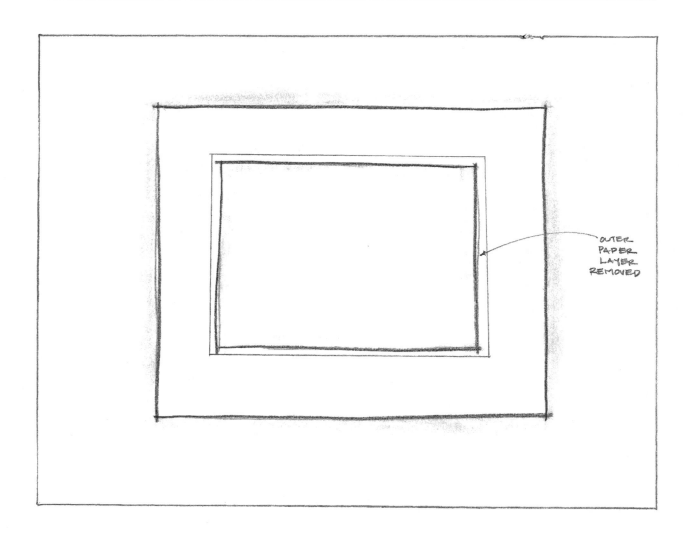

OUTER
PAPER
LAYER
REMOVED

STEP 9

To attach the sketch, place a piece of tape—sticky
side up—at each corner of the sketch.

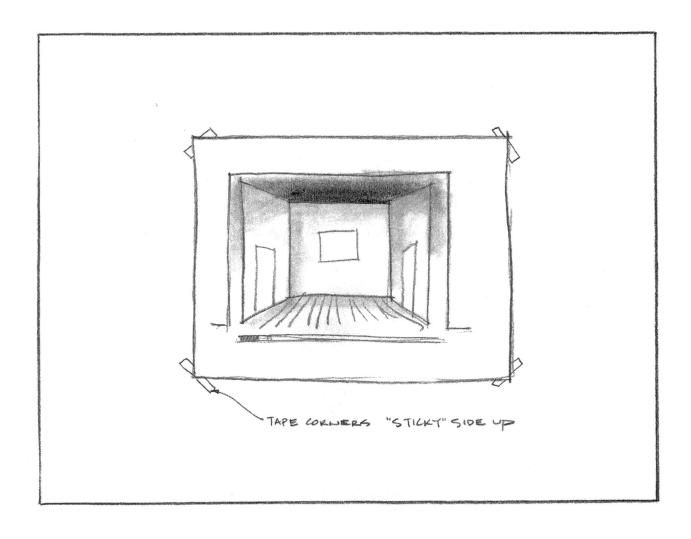

TAPE CORNERS "STICKY" SIDE UP

STEP 10

Position the matt over the sketch on a hard surface. When the alignment is right, press down on the matt. Gently turn the matt and sketch over and complete the taping job. You can get a more finished look by attaching a sheet of craft paper or chip board to the back of the matt board. This covers and protects the back of your sketch and cleans up your presentation.

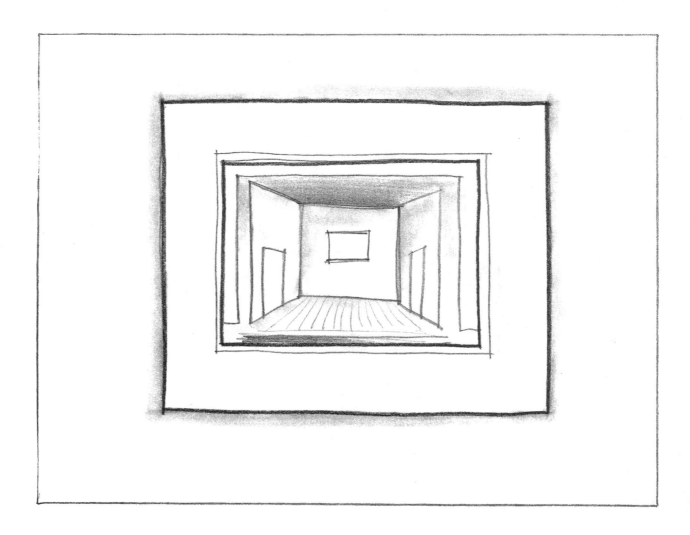

15

A Portfolio of Sketches

SURVEY TECHNIQUES AND MATERIALS

This chapter provides a few sketch examples. The techniques vary in materials and in the "finished" (or not-so-finished) quality of the sketches. Take note of the range. These are not beautiful pieces of art, but that is not their purpose. Instead, they communicate ideas to directors and designers. Some of the sketches include writing and others include floor plans. Some are final sketches or renderings, and others seem quite "sketchy." The point here is that the sketch is a prop that helps you and the other production team members engage in a dialogue about the play, film or television production.

SKETCH FOR *IN THE SWEET BYE AND BYE*

This sketch was drawn on tracing paper in ink. It is actually a tracing of a slightly rougher pencil sketch. A "second-generation" ink sketch was used to help identify elements of the set dressing. The show is a realistic "kitchen sink" comedy. The set dressing and properties are specific to the action. It was felt that ink could spell the specific references to these items better than a rough pencil sketch could.

SKETCH FOR *FOUND A PEANUT*

Pencil on newsprint was used for this sketch. In this design the set extended above to the lights and into the audience. These elements were then included in the sketch to let the director and the other production team members get a sense of what this encroachment might look like in the theater.

SKETCH FOR *ANYONE CAN WHISTLE*

Pencil on tracing paper was used here. This sketch presents a quick foliage technique.

SKETCH FOR *HENRY V, PART IV*

This very quick sketch was done in pencil on sketch paper (bond). Notice the simple rendering of plat-forms, wood and shading.

SKETCH FOR *TRAILS*

Another sketch in pencil on sketch paper. The set is composed of clear Plexiglas units mounted on a steel framework. The squares in the background are rear projection screens. Notice the diagonal lines used to represent a reflective surface.

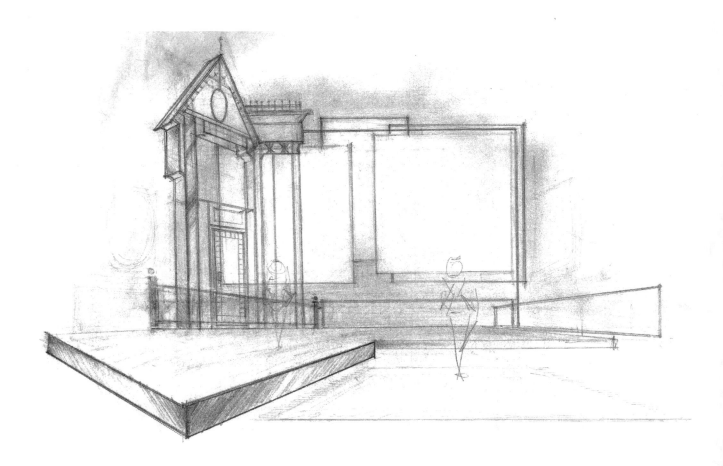

RENDERING FOR *THE BOYFRIEND*

This final sketch was done in pencil on tracing paper
and was drawn just prior to rendering the design in
color.

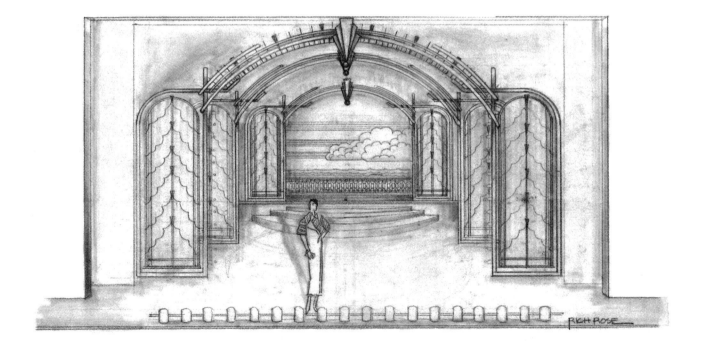

The Last Word

The sketching skills that you have surveyed in these pages can help you communicate more productively as a designer. Of course, all of this generates from a good design — a design that you can see in your head but can't quite translate to paper. This book is about crossing the bridge that connects your ideas with your drawings. A convincing communication of your design in the early sketch stage also means you are telling the story beyond the basic facts of what goes where. You are providing the director and other designers with important information about the use of space, the tone of the play and even about the characters whose stories will unfold in this setting.

Getting the most from your communication skills starts with discovering the system that works for you. Try all of the methods described in this book. You will likely settle on the one that "feels right." It should be a system that you understand intuitively and allows you to work rapidly. You should feel comfortable laying in the next layer — assigning the details and textures that will tell so much about the inhabitants of this world. Although the sketch may typically look finished once you have laid in the details, don't neglect to add the last layer — atmosphere and shading. Shading permits your two-dimensional sketch to look three-dimensional. This is important for understanding the use of space, and it is the key to convincing the members of the production team that your vision of the play is worth pursuing. Only with this last step is your sketch truly complete.

Take each of these steps one at a time and begin to master them. Soon you will discover that you can draw *complete* sketches that look closer and closer to that idea in your head while spending less time doing so. In the first chapter I discussed a sketch diary. I can't recommend this highly enough. A sketch diary is the best, and perhaps only way to build your drawing muscles. From creating perspective technique to rendering textures to layering in atmosphere — the more techniques you tackle in your sketch diary, the more natural they will all become. Experience is your tutor now. Never be content. I invite you to accept that each new project becomes yet another lesson from which to discover new skills, methods and abilities.

INDEX